THE NEW LEGALITY

In the Light of the Christian

Philosophy of Law

By
Hebden Taylor

PRESBYTERIAN AND REFORMED PUBLISHING COMPANY
PHILADELPHIA, PA.
1967

UNIVERSITY SERIES: *Historical Studies*

Rousas J. Rushdoony, *Editor*

THE AUTHOR

The Reverend E. L. Hebden Taylor was born of medical missionary parents in Katanga, Belgium Congo, in 1925. Educated in English schools, he graduated from Trinity Hall, Cambridge University, with honors in 1949, and in 1952 received his Licentiate in Theology from the Anglican Theological College of British Columbia at Vancouver, Canada.

During the Second World War he served in the Royal Navy on the H.S.M. Diadem. He served as a missionary among the trappers and Yukon Indians on the Alaskan Highway (1952-1954). Since then he has had pastorates at St. Matthew's Church, Hampstead, Montreal; Holy Trinity Church, Langley, England, and is currently the Vicar of Greegates, Bradford, Yorkshire, England.

The Reverend Taylor is well known in England and Canada as a lecturer and author. Periodicals to which he has frequently contributed include *His Dominion, The Canadian Churchman, The Canadian Bar Journal*, the *Canadian Medical Association Journal*, the *Queen's University Quarterly*, and the *Canadian Legionary Magazine*. He has been active in behalf of the Christian Labour Association of Canada, the Christian Action Movement, and the Ontario Committee for Christian Political Action.

He is the author of the recently published monumental 600 page *The Christian Philosophy of Law, Politics, and the State*, a comprehensive study of the philosophy of Herman Dooyeweerd. (It is available through our order department.)

CONTENTS

HUMANISTIC LAW

The dictionary definition of law is, basically, that law is "1. A rule of action established by recognized authority to enforce justice and prescribe duty or obligation; a legislative enactment. 2. A system of rules or regulations recognized by men or nations or applied in courts of law." According to Kant, "Every formula which expresses the necessity of an action is called a law."

These are ostensibly definitions. They are actually evasions. A definition explains, cites the limits of something, or shows what the contexts of a conception are. But law cannot be explained, it cannot be defined, without reference to religion. Law is concerned with matters of justice, authority, duty, and obligation, all matters of religious concern and inescapably involved with matters of "ultimate concern."

Ostensibly, in our secular culture, religion has been separated from law, and law is now purely a matter of sociological concerns, oriented to social needs and progressively scientific criteria rather than to religious dogma. Actually, however, our law is thoroughly religious and is directly a product of religion. *Note*

The separation of religion from law is rather the separation of Christianity from law. Christianity has for centuries been the major impetus to legal codes, and Western law has been a manifestation of changing and developing currents of Christian philosophy and theology. · Now, however, Christianity is in radical and revolutionary process of disestablishment as the religious foundation of laws, states, and civil governments, and it is being steadily replaced by another religion, the religion of humanity or humanism. (The fact that humanism is a non-theistic faith does not make it any the less a religion. Indeed, almost all the religions of the world have been non-theistic. Buddhism is clearly non-theistic, as are the Hindu religions. Taoism is non-theistic, as are the many primitive religions of

v

the world. The presence of gods in many religions of antiquity did not conceal the fact that ultimacy did not belong to these gods. They were, like men, products of the universe; blind chaos ruled as ultimate in the past and in the future. The fact that religious sentiment has moved again towards a non-theistic faith does not make that faith any the less religion. Religion is more often to be identified as non-theistic than theistic, and it can be argued that there is no true theism apart from Christian or Biblical theism, and that an ultimate decree is only ascribed to God in truly Biblical theism.

Humanism is today a world-wide religious force. It is increasingly the religious force motivating legislation on every continent and in every state of the world, and humanism is established on a world-wide basis as the religious motive of the United Nations. The United Nations Charter is as much a religious document and manifesto as it is a document of world law. From start to finish, it is expressive of the humanistic religious ideal to a far greater extent than it is legal reality. Not only is humanism the established religion of the United Nations, it is also an intolerant and exclusive religion, in that no right of existence is theoretically granted to any discrimination with respect to "creed." No creedal expression of religion is permitted other than humanism. Other religions can exist only if they become humanistic, only, for example, if Christianity divests itself of its Bibical faith and becomes a vehicle for humanism. In every area of the world there is steady pressure against Christianity and continued attempts to abolish "discrimination" as to creed by making the humanistic creed the standard of all law with respect to religion, the state, and morality. We are in the midst of a world-wide humanistic legal revolution which is even more radical than the bloody revolutions of humanism.

Humanistic law, moreover, is inescapably totalitarian law. Humanism, as the logical development of evolutionary theory, holds fundamentally to a concept of an evolving universe. This is held to be a concept of an "open universe," whereas Biblical Christianity, because of its faith in the triune God and His eternal decree, is said to be a faith in a "closed universe." This terminology not only intends to prejudice the case; it reverses reality. The universe of evolution and humanism is a closed universe. There is no law, no appeal, no higher order, beyond and above the universe. Instead of an

vi

open window upwards, there is a closed cosmos. (There is thus no ultimate law and decree beyond man and the universe.\ Man's law is therefore beyond criticism except by man.) In practice, this means that the positive law of the state is absolute law. (The state is the most powerful and most highly organized expression of humanistic man, and the state is the form over the universe, over every human order, the law of the state is a closed system of law.\ There is no appeal beyond it. Man has no "right," no realm of justice, no source of law beyond the state, to which he can appeal against the state. Humanism therefore imprisons man within the closed world of the state and the closed universe of the evolutionary scheme.

From the Biblical perspective, man is a creature of God, was created in His image and was called to be king over creation under God and priest and prophet therein. (In Jesus Christ, man dead in sins and trespasses, is restored and enabled to fulfil his creation mandate.) For Christian man, the universe is an open one: he has an appeal to God against the tyranny of a sinful, lawless state, and he has the certainty of triumph because of God's absolute Kingship. The world is the dominion of the Christian man, a realm in which he is the predestined monarch, commissioned to subdue the earth and exercise dominion over it. For humanistic man, the world is a prison house, a closed world in which the unlimited state bangs shut the door of man's cell and leaves man in solitary confinement, without appeal against the state because there is no higher law over the state. The state's law is absolute law, only the state can correct the law of the state, and, at any given point, the law of the state is beyond appeal. The law of the humanistic state is the infallible word of the state for the moment in history. (There is no supreme court of God beyond the state to negate or judge the state.)

But this is not all. The humanistic state not only lacks a transcendental limitation on its law, it also lacks all such limitations on its *power,* so that its total power reinforces its total law. The state thus unites absolute power to absolute jurisdiction and it inevitably claims absolute competence. *Note*

The claim to absolute competence grows progressively with the claims to absolute power and absolute jurisdiction. As the state intrudes into one area after another, its claims to competence grow simultaneously with its claim to jurisdiction and with its controls.

lying beyond the limits of experience

The state claims to be the arbiter of the common good and the means to realizing the common good. Accordingly, religion, economics, health, welfare, education, agriculture, forestry, science, geriatrics, and all things else become aspects of the activity and concern of the state. The state has assumed the role of God and claims the omnicompetence of God, and accordingly it has a "necessary" function in every realm as the new god of being.

Moreover, the state as the new god of being, assumes the necessary responsibility of God, an eternal decree, predestination or total planning. Planning commissions and state planning become central functions of the state, and master plans are established for every sphere, vocation, and area of man's life and for the natural world. The state as god replaces God's eternal decree with the state's total plan.

God as God is above His law; God is not good because He conforms to a good higher than Himself, but rather He is good because His nature is itself true righteousness and holiness, and God is true to Himself. There is no criterion above God; the laws of creation and the laws of religion and morality are expressions of His nature, will, and purpose. They are determined by God and are revelatory of Him.

When the humanistic state, in terms of the nature of its being, claims absolute competence, it claims thereby that it is itself above the law. The state therefore stands above its citizens and above its own law as its own justification. But, since the essential nature of the humanistic state, which has no law above itself, is *power,* and it maintains itself in terms of *power,* its basic law is *power.* The basic and essential self-determination of the humanistic state is thus in terms of *power.* Even as the sovereign God's holiness and righteousness express His being, so the sovereign state's *power* expresses its being. The humanistic state may profess the common good, democracy, equality, fraternity, and much else, but it moves essentially and always in terms of power, or else it finds lean and hungry humanistic wolves ready to devour it. The noble professions of the humanistic state are therefore essentially a sugar-coating of the power-pill. If the state moves to "remedy" infirm and aged pensioners' problems, the real gainer is the state: the move steadily results in a minimum of advantage to the pensioners, and the maximum of power for the state. In every sphere into which the state intrudes, the results are the same. The state gains and the people lose. The gain and the loss are in the same area: liberty and power, the state gains the liberty and power lost by the people.

The humanistic state, because its claim is to universal jurisdiction, is thereby a competitor to and a supplanter of the various law spheres and of man. (It gains power by robbing power) It gains power over the economic sphere, and over education, by robbing economics of liberty and power, and by usurping the independence of education. (The humanistic state, instead of being a benefactor of its people, is their powerful competitor and supplanter. (It can only prosper by displacing man and man's legitimate activities. The state thus seeks to supplant both God and man.)

Basically, the humanistic state is simply the organizataion and control of the legislative or judicial powers. ("Right" is therefore what the state does, and what the state does is to develop, consolidate, and extend its power, and the positive law of the state is the formalization of this power. It is the absolutization of the state.

Too often, the only alternative presented to this absolutizing of the state is the absolutization of the individual. The atomistic individual is exalted to a position of ultimacy and becomes his own new god, his own ultimate arbiter of good and evil.

Anarchism together with statism presupposes an unfallen and normative world, and hence it seeks a normative and absolute standard from that world. This standard may be the individual or the collective man; it may be natural law; it may be reason, or a number of other things. It still remains defective and false, *first,* in that an aspect of creation is given a creative and absolute role, and, *second,* in that the fallen and sinful creation and creature is held to be normative and the source therefore of the god.

In view of the obvious evils of humanistic law, it is all the more urgent that not only Biblical Christianity be recognized as the only true foundation of law and of the state, but that the Biblical concept of law be explored. This is a major task, and one long overdue. The foundations for this re-examination have been brilliantly studied in recent years by Herman Dooyeweerd, and they have been described by his many associates and followers. In this country, the foundations have been delineated from the perspective of the philosophy of religion by Cornelius Van Til.

In E. L. Hebden Taylor's study, we have an able introduction to the subject, and a studied challenge *to* the "new legality." It deserves extensive attention.

Rousas John Rushdoony
Woodland Hills, California

THE NEW LEGALITY

1. The Challenge of the New Legality

In the important books, *Life, Death and the Law* by Dr. N. St. John-Stevas and *The Sanctity of Life and the Criminal Law* by Dr. Glanville Williams, it is shown that it is in the name of secular humanist psychology, anthropology and sociology that we are being asked to legalize homosexuality, prostitution, gambling, suicide, abortion, artificial insemination of women, sterilization of the unfit and euthanasia. All these radical demands for changes in the existing criminal laws forbidding such practices reflect the immense changes in public opinion that have taken place in the English-speaking world largely as the result of the penetration and conquest of our universities, schools, press, churches, and political parties by the militant minority of "scientific humanists."

The appeal in every case to amend the existing laws, whether it be labelled humanitarian, liberal or utilitarian, is to the supposed new "scientific" insights into the human situation and human nature which secular social science and psychiatry claims to have provided. Hence the demand for legal recognition of the new anthropology, morality and legality of non-Christian humanists and for legislation that would implement them.

This new legality based upon man's declaration of independence from God and His creation ordinances and structures has been advocated in a number of recent secular humanist documents, e.g., The Cadogan Report on Corporal Punishment, The Kinsey Report on Sex, the Wolfenden Report on Prostitution and Homosexuality, the Report of the Royal Commission on Capital Punishment, The Reports of the Departmental Committees on Artificial Insemination and on Abortion.

That all these questions are now being forced upon our notice is due to the fact that the attitude of the community—fairly unanimous until comparatively recent times and governed largely by theological beliefs and moral values commanding almost universal acceptance—has undergone a significant secular revolution. New biological, phychological and sociological knowledge has breached the phalanx of public opinion deeply. Having supposedly defeated the Word of God over the riddles of the universe, secular scientists now seek to usurp the role of Christian anthropology, morality and law in deciding how we should organize our legal system and "treat" our socially "maladjusted" citizens.

Given this new situation Christians can expect to be increasingly confronted with laws to which their conscience cannot subscribe, and they will perhaps be tempted to look back to a social order in which the moral law had its inexorable sanctions. As St. John-Stevas sees it, the emergence of the pluralist society, in which tolerance must be the guarantee of any social peace, means that Christian moral teaching must commend itself by its inherent worth and not by reliance on external penalties. Such a tension can in fact be creative of good, he suggests, but it must spring from an informed awareness of the true roots of morality and law which are to be found not merely in the arbitrary dictates of ecclesiastical authority but in a consistent understanding of the nature and rights of man and hence in the moral law that defines his authentic needs. As he views it:

> The basic struggle is not the relation of Church and State but the relation of Church and Society. Society cannot be redeemed by the coercive will imposed through the instrumentality of the state, but by the individual spurred to action by persuasion.[1]

2. The Church's Accommodation with Legal Humanism

It is significant that St. John-Stevas views this struggle between the old and the new legality in *moral* terms. As a Roman Catholic he thinks of "law" as part of a larger embracing whole, which Roman Catholic theory has defined as the Natural Law. For Roman Catholics all legal, political and social questions hinge upon what Pope Pius XI called "the entire moral law" in the encyclical *Quadragesimo Anno*.

Roman Catholics do not seem to realize that the coming of Christ has not only brought about a radical change of heart in individuals but also in direction of man's social and political structures. The Bible clearly indicates that redemption is not confined to individuals but involves the whole creation. Roman Catholics on the other hand accept the fallen structures of society as being natural and not radically affected by man's original and actual sin. As a result Roman Catholic social reconstruction turns out to be no true re-formation of society at all but at most a re-

2

direction of things as they are naturally given, or a super-addition of Roman Catholic social science on to the social structures as they stand. The Roman Catholic therefore in principle does not reform or attempt to reform the state or society in the light of God's Word nor from a scriptural sense of the structure of reality. Instead he largely accepts the values and institutions of society as these have developed in the historical experience of the western world. He seeks a solution of the legal and social problems in terms of the Natural Moral Law and reform proceeds largely by way of synthesis and accommodation of this Natural Law with unredeemed human institutions. Such a method of cultural accommodation finds its origin in the teachings of medieval scholasticism and especially of Thomas Aquinas, who synthesized Greek and Christian basic presuppositions about man's nature, origin and destiny.

Nature, conceived as form and matter in the Greek sense becomes for Aquinas the autonomous basis of supernatural grace. By means of his doctrine of the eternal law, with its subjective counterpart in the natural law, Aquinas sought to accommodate the Greek form matter motive with the biblical ground motive of creation, the fall into sin, and redemption through Jesus Christ in the communion of the Holy Spirit. Through the natural law the creation, in its essential nature, has a subjective part in the eternal law of God's world plan. Such a synthesis of the biblical and Greek religious ground motives implied a distinction between a natural and a supernatural sphere of thought and action. Within the sphere of nature a relative autonomy was ascribed by Aquinas to human reason which he supposed to be capable by its own unaided light of discovering the natural truths about the universe and of man's social life within it. As David Knowles writes in *The Evolution of Medieval Thought*:

> Aquinas accepted human reason as an adequate and self-sufficient instrument for attaining truth within the realm of man's natural experience, and in so doing gave, not only to abstract thought but to all scientific knowledge, rights of citizenship in a Christian world. He accepted in its main lines the system of Aristotle as a basis for his own interpretation of the visible universe, and this acceptance did not exclude the ethical and political teaching of the Philosopher. By so doing, and without a full realization of all the consequences,

3

Thomas admitted into the Christian purview all the natural values of human social activity.[2]

According to Aquinas reason and revelation, human nature and the supernatural values revealed in the Bible are fundamentally in harmony. In his own famous words, "Grace does not abolish nature but perfects it." Such a formula expresses not only an entirely new interpretation of the relationship between reason and revelation, but also a new conception of the capacities of human nature and of the effect of sin upon it. As another Roman Catholic writer A. P. d'Entreves points out in his book, *Aquinas' Selected Writings*:

> This formula expresses an entirely different attitude to life from the diffidence and hostility of earlier Christian thought. St. Thomas' assertion, that grace does not abolish nature but perfects it implies that human values and truths are not necessarily obliterated by the revelation of higher ones; however modest and low, they deserve to be considered as possible tools for the great task of building up a Christian civilization. It also implies the recognition of the existence and dignity of a purely "natural" sphere of rational and ethical values.[3]

Aquinas taught that sin had merely removed certain supernatural gifts from man, but left his human nature and reason intact. Before the Fall man was endowed with such supernatural gifts, whereby he was not merely righteous, pure and untempted, but also enjoyed a measure of God's own divine nature and goodness. It was this super-added gift of grace which Adam lost by his sin. Thus for Aquinas, man after the Fall retained the image of God, which consists in his freedom and rationality of his nature, but lost his likeness to God, which consists in his self-determination according to his divine destiny.

Upon this sub-biblical doctrine of human nature, Aquinas now proceeded to erect not only his theology and anthropology but also his sociology and doctrines of law and the state and theory of culture.

If human nature is really such as Thomas supposed, what need has man for God's grace and help at all? Why bother bringing God into the human picture at all if man is already perfectly rational and capable of achieving his own destiny and realizing his own potentialities in this world? If man can bring in or build or otherwise

4

provide a kingdom for God, why bother bringing God into the picture at all?

Instead of conceiving of the state as God's appointed method of restraining human sinfulness as Paul and Augustine had taught, Aquinas and succeeding Roman Catholic thinkers proceeded to give a purely natural, that is, rational, explanation of man's social institutions.

As Professor d'Entreves writes in his book *Natural Law* concerning Aquinas' dictum, "Grace does not abolish nature but perfects it":

> It was a momentous discovery, for it made it possible to accept the Aristotelian conception of ethics and politics and to graft it, as it were, on the Christian interpretation of life.[4]

As a direct and tragic result of this accommodation there was no longer felt any need for a distinctive Christian philosophy of law, politics and the State. The social sciences as well as the natural sciences were in fact abandoned to the influence of the Greek pagan religious ground motives in their external accommodation to the Christian doctrines of man in society. In his fundamental work *The Growth of Papal Government in the Middle Ages*, Walter Ullmann points out that:

> The impact of Aristotle on the late medieval world is not only . . . of importance to mere philosophic enquiries, but also, and we venture to say of greater importance in the field of political science. There are indeed two different worlds, that before and that after the Aristotelian absorption. . . . Aristotle had shown . . . that there was a *societas humana*, the aim of which was the satisfaction of human needs. This *societas humana* is something fundamentally different from the *societas christiana*. It grows from below . . . and it is therefore a creation of nature. The *societas christiana* comes, so to speak, from above . . . it has therefore its origin outside nature (page 455).

After Aquinas the tendency increased to elucidate the first principles of social, political and legal science without any reference whatsoever to the principles of God's Word and Law for human society. Why bother bringing revelation into the picture at all if human reason can discover the principles governing the *societas humana*? If man can of his own rational faculties and by means of

5

his scientific method build a successful social and legal order, why bring religion into life?

While Aquinas himself never drew such unchristian conclusions, it did not take his successors at French, German, Italian, and British universities long to do so. Such a process of the secularization of the social sciences or the humanities as they were then called inevitably developed out of the distinction first drawn by Aquinas between the order of faith and the order of natural reason.

One of the great tragedies of the Protestant Reformation was the failure of the Reformers to reverse this secularizing process in legal and political thought by developing a doctrine of law, politics and the state upon truly biblical and reformed lines. The Reformers did not bring about any radical departures in the spheres of political science and jurisprudence for the simple reason, as August Lang showed in his essay *The Reformation and Natural Law*,[5] that they were so involved in theological disputes, religious controversy and the very struggle for survival that they simply did not have any time left in which to develop a truly scriptural view of law and politics.

Luther confused things by his doctrine of the higher and lower realms. Calvin did bring the two realms of grace and nature as closely together as he could in his thinking. The main error set in during the second and third generation of the Reformation when a new Protestant accommodation with Aristotelianism took place in the thinking of such men as Peter Ramus, Melanchton, Thomas Beza and then later during the seventeenth century in the work of the Cambridge Platonists, the Dutch Reformed theologians and American Puritans such as Roger Williams.

Having failed to re-define the basic postulates of jurisprudence in terms of the Reformation view of man, succeeding generations of Protestants have been unable to withstand the onrush of the new secular humanist conceptions of law which emerged in such men as Hobbes, Locke, Grotius, Bentham, Mill and more recently Pound, Stone, Dicey, Wooton and Hart.

Modern so called "progressive" thought has corrupted Christians to such an extent as Harry Blamires says there is no longer a "Christian Mind." Today Christians no longer depend upon

6

the Word of God for a unified directive in matters relating to law and politics. The Church Assembly Board for Social Responsibility has produced a report on Punishment which bends over backwards to accommodate itself to the new legality. The General Council of the United Church of Canada in 1960 accepted the Report of its Council for Social Responsibility on Crime and Punishment. Amongst other things this calls for the abolition of the death penalty and it suggests that courts should in the future only decide the guilt or innocence of a person and that convicted criminals should be sent to hospitals and clinics rather than places of punishment. It argues in favor of these proposals:

> We contend that as most serious offences are symptomatic of social or psychological aberrations, the treatment of the offender should be determined by a diagnostic investigation which should be an integral part of a treatment process commencing *before* trial and ending with the ultimate emancipation of the offender from his criminality. We suggest that the present method of meting out punishment is no longer compatible with enlightened Christian and sociological thinkings.

In legal matters it would thus seem that the majority of English-speaking Protestants now accept as axiomatic the doctrine that no so-called sectarian dogma shall function as the foundation of modern legal discussion. It is assumed as a matter of course that there is a realm of supposedly neutral scientific thought which can without loss to Christian principles be shared in common with secular humanists. By accepting such a doctrine the Christian community is rendering itself powerless to influence the direction now being taken by legal and political life in the English-speaking world. Having restricted their religion to their churches and homes, Protestants as citizens have freed themselves from the reforming power of God's Word to accept whatever their non-Christian fellow citizens find "reasonable" and "scientific." In consequence there has taken place the revolutionary secularization of all other social spheres. Any idea that Christians ought to try to bring the legal and political areas of life into conformity with God's creation norms has disappeared.

This abdication of responsibility is at the root of the spiritual crisis facing us today which can only effectively be resolved when enough Christians recover the biblical view of religion as the fundamental predicament of *all* human beings. Before Christians can hope to expound a truly scriptural view of law, morality and society they must recover the biblical insight that *life is religion*, not morality nor science. Before we can talk significantly about man's political or legal life we must first know what life itself is. Is life morality as Roman Catholics suppose, or is it reason and science as humanists suppose? The Word of God makes it clear that man's life is fundamentally religion, the service of the one true God Who has revealed Himself in the Bible or of an idol or false god of man's own devising. Human life as created by God is religion. For this reason the opposite of true religion is never described in the Bible as atheism or neutralism but as idolatry; while unbelief is described not as the absence of faith, but always as misdirected faith in a false god or idol. Man is that being who has been created *responsible*, i.e., answerable to God for all his actions and to whom he must render an account of all his doings and ways. Hence the Bible defines man as *homo religiosus*, a religious being, not as *homo faber* or *homo sapiens*, a tool making or rational being.

3. The Reformed Response to the New Legality In the Christian Philosophy of the Cosmonomic Law-Idea

If life is religion it follows that we need an approach to the new legality which is radically based on our faith in God's sovereignty over the *whole* of human life and in God's Word written in the Scriptures. as the *ordering principle* of all our theoretical as well as practical activities; an approach which grows out of the central radical illumination that the Word of God works in our hearts. For the Bible does not offer merely pietistic recipes and moral imperatives for limited areas of life. It does not give merely moral direction; it gives *direction* for the whole of life.

No one has seen this more clearly in our generation than Herman Dooyeweerd, Professor Emeritus of the History and Philosophy of Law at the Free University, Amsterdam. A truly Christian theory of law and society he says must be based on a renewed biblical religious insight into the divinely established structural principles of human society and not upon theology as such, which can be of little help in solving legal problems. He holds that there must be a directly biblical and not an indirectly *theological* reformation of thought and action.

Dooyeweerd finds the point of departure for all truly Christian theoretical thought in the biblical ground motive or basic presupposition of the creation of the world by God, the fall of man into sin, and the redemption of man by Jesus Christ in the communion of the Holy Spirit.

Now one of the most important facts the Bible reveals is that God is the true and original architect of the Universe and that He has placed his entire creation under law. Without this law everything would collapse into chaos. For the Bible that which defines the antichrist, the man of sin, the godless man is precisely his will to live without law (II Thess. 11: 3-8).

The term cosmonomic law order as Dooyeweerd uses it expresses the fact that everything created is subject to the laws of God. He speaks of a law-order because he recognizes a multiplicity of divine laws established by the Creator in a specific order.

Law is the boundary line dividing God from the cosmos. God is above law; everything else is subject to law. The idea of law can thus never be separated from the idea of the source of law in God's sovereign will and the idea of the subject of law. Law and subject are correlative terms.

Dooyeweerd does not conceive of the notion of law in a purely juridical or moral sense. God's laws are not confined to the Decalogue. They must be seen primarily as universal ordinances and uniformities encompassing creation in all its aspects as constant structural principles making possible individual things and events. Their ontological character is guaranteed by the fact that they are not founded in the subjective consciousness, but are created by God.

According to Dooyeweerd every part of creation belongs to a different law-sphere and so creation exhibits as many aspects as there are law-spheres. In his way he leads us into his theory of the modal spheres which is developed from his doctrine of the sovereignty of God by means of his theory of cosmic time, which "constitutes the basis of the philosophical theory of reality."[6] In order

9

to explain his meaning more fully Dooyeweerd makes use of a figure:

> The light of the sun is refracted through a prism, and this refraction is perceived by the eye of sense in the seven well-known colours of the spectrum. In themselves all colours are dependent refractions of the unrefracted light, and none of them can be regarded as an integral of the colour differentiation. Further not one of the seven colours is capable of existing in the spectrum apart from its coherence with the rest, and by the interception of the unrefracted light the entire play of colours vanishes into nothing.
>
> The unrefracted light is the time-transcending totality of meaning of our cosmos with respect to cosmonomic side and its subject side. As this light has its origin in the source of light, so the totality of meaning of our cosmos has its origin in its arche through whom and to whom it has been created.
>
> The prism that achieves the refraction of colour is cosmic time, through which the religious fulness of meaning is broken up into its temporal modal aspects of meaning.
>
> As the seven colours do not owe their origin to one another, so the temporal aspects of meaning in the face of each other have sphere sovereignty or modal irreducibility.
>
> In the religious fulness of meaning there is but one law of God just as there is but one sin against God, and one mankind which has sinned in Adam. But under the boundary line of time, this fulness of meaning with reference to its cosmonomic side as well as its subject separates, like the sunlight through the prism, into a rich variation of modal aspects of meaning. Each modal aspect is sovereign in its own sphere, and each aspect in its modal structure reflects the fulness of meaning in its own modality.[7]

Through cosmic time God's sovereign, undivided law-structure of creation is therefore broken up or refracted into a number of modes of time, modes of meaning or modal spheres. The structure for creation has these various "moments" which make possible the various aspects of reality, the different ways in which reality exists and functions. Thus we are all immediately aware of the difference between an economic act such as the purchase of a book, and an act of thought, such as reading the book's contents. Science does not create these law-spheres nor are they first distinguished by science. While all aspects of reality are intuitively encountered in direct "naive" experience, in science this encounter is deepened into a theoretical insight into the various law-spheres. (See diagram of Dooyeweerd's cosmology in Appendix.)

God's creation, subject to his divinely established structure thus exists in various law-spheres. Dooyeweerd has so far distinguished fifteen of these spheres. They are the numerical and the spatial studied by mathematics, the physical studied by physics and chemistry, the biological studied by biology and medicine, the psychical studied by psychology, the analytical studied in logic, the historical-cultural studied in history, the linguistic studied by philology and semantics, the social studied by sociology, the economic studied in economics, the aesthetic studied by aesthetics, the juridical studied in jurisprudence, the ethical studied by ethics and the faith aspect studied by theology.

These law-spheres are the ways in which reality exists and so they are called by Dooyeweerd modes or modalities. Since these never appear as separate entities but are always sides of individual things, he calls them aspects. Since they appear only with things existing in time, he calls them functions. These modes must not be confused with Kant's categories of thought, Kant's so-called transcendental postulates. And they are irreducible and thus they cannot be brought back to more basic modes, as is done for example in rationalism, in which the aspects which are higher than the logical are considered as mere constructions postulated by the abstracting human mind. Similar reductions can be found in historicism in which all reality is subsumed under the category of historical modes of thought (cf. R. G. Collingwood, *The Idea of Nature*) or in Marx's economic man.

Since these aspects are "ontic" and cannot be reduced to each other, we can speak of the relationship of these aspects as "sovereign within their own spheres." Each sphere possesses its own laws independently of the other spheres. Each sphere of existence has received from God its own peculiar nature and, as Genesis says, is "created each after its own kind." The capacities of one sphere may not be transferred or appropriated by another sphere.

Dooyeweerd here acknowledges his debt to Kuyper's application of the scriptural principle of God's universal sovereignty to philosophy. Each sphere has a status, rooted in its divinely instituted nature, which cannot be infringed upon by any other sphere. This

11

constitutes its modal sovereignty, or sovereignty in its own orbit, and in virtue of which each modal sphere is equal. Thus we must not base the law-sphere on the moral sphere. Both law and ethics are "independent" expressions of the created order which in essence is religious, not moral.

The theory of modalities breaks with the traditional Western legal thought which viewed "law" in its legal sense as part of a larger embracing whole which was then termed the moral order or the Natural Moral Law.

This does not mean that law and morality are separate, but the order is a reversed one. In the life of the law of the state there must be a moral deepening and anticipation.

According to Dooyeweerd every modality or law-sphere is an intrinsic part of the total structure of reality and is a reflection of the religious fulness of meaning; consequently the temporal order of the modal spheres must be expressed in each sphere. This fact must be recognized by the specialist in every particular field of human science. For in every special science the fundamental concepts are formulated only when the modal moment of the specific modality which is being studied is seen in its relation and coherence to the other modalities or law-spheres. This aspect of the Christian philosophy of law enables Dooyeweerd to develop a Christian jurisprudence in close relation to the other sciences and areas of human life and so to avoid the pitfalls of rationalistic reductionism.

Dooyeweerd maintains that the fundamental concepts of jurisprudence are formulated by the analogies between the modalities which "precede" the juridical (the numerical through to the aesthetic law-spheres) and the juridical modality itself.

He distinguishes between the concept of justice and the idea of justice. The former is formulated by discovering the analogies between the lower modalities and the juridical modality. The latter is formulated by discovering the relation between law and the higher functions, namely those of ethics and faith.

In its relation to the lower aspects of reality Dooyeweerd would have us think of the legal modality in its restrictive function. If legal life develops only in relation to these aspects, then it remains closed, e.g., the primitive idea of corporate personality and the ancient custom of blood vengeance against the whole clan,

12

family or tribe to which the individual murderer belonged. But as soon as law develops in relation to morality and faith, then he claims we discover a deepening of legal life, e.g., the principle of equity is a moral deepening of legal rules so that the individual factor can be given a greater play; the introduction of the notion of guilt into criminal law and the protection of the Habeas Corpus Acts are all moral refractions upon the law (cf. N. Micklem, *The Law and the Laws*, London, 1952).

4. *The Meaning of Law*

Dooyeweerd distinguishes between the normative and the a-normative spheres. By this he means that the subjects of the first five spheres have no option but to obey their correlative laws. From the analytical sphere onwards, however, the laws become *norms*. Although these norms have been laid down by God in principle in the structure of each sphere, they must be discovered and applied or positivised. Thus the laws of justice or love, for example, do not contain a precise formulation of their meaning in each concrete instance. Jurisprudence is thus a normative science.

Accordingly law may be defined as a complex of norms, regulating the relations between men and human institutions by means of a careful balancing of their interests, in conformity with the social structures as given in the Creation.

The divine order for human society manifests itself in a great variety of specific creation structures or ordinances. All these ordinances not only find their origin in God but they are also continually upheld by His omnipotence and providence. In Him they find their ultimate purpose. They are the instruments of His common grace and providence through which the Sovereign Lord executes His Lordship over the creation and activates human life along stable ways. In and with these ordinances God confronts man. That is to say they are not a natural "datum" like the natural laws of physics, but rather they are laid upon man to be realized in history, to be positivised. Or, to put it another way, God calls man into His service as his co-worker in the realization of the social order. Human culture is the fulfillment of the great cultural mandate given to man at the beginning of his history, "Replenish the earth and subdue it and have dominion over it" (Gen. 1:28).

13

The social ordinances given by God are laws of structure which determine the task of the various relations of life. Thus the family, the church as an institution and the state are ruled by their own divinely willed order or structure, whether or not those who are involved in these social groupings acknowledge this order. Each of these communities stands in this world with a specific task, which cannot be arbitrarily changed by man without him suffering loss. Each of these communities or associations which have emerged in the course of history, e.g., the business enterprise, the university, the trade union, the church, displays a constant structure, and is its own specific structure or law which it cannot negate without suffering loss.

The norms governing these social structures form one whole, in spite of their great variety. But what is it that makes these norms into one whole, one complex? It is the fact that all these norms can be traced back to one and the same origin. They have been established by the Creator for man's life in this world, which is a created world. God has laid down these norms as the directives along which life in this world should be conducted.

Man, however, has been created as a responsible being and must therefore from these directives discover the norms that should apply in his daily life; for the Creator gives directives only, not rules for concrete situations. This means at the same time, however, that man may fail by not discovering or obeying these norms.

Man, therefore, thanks to his capacity for reasoning with which he has been endowed by the Creator, discovers the norms that are valid for this life from the directives given by God. This means, however, that they are of a temporary nature, that they are anchored in the existence of this world. If man were to proceed and establish unalterable, external norms valid at all times and places, as advocated by prophets of the Natural Law School, he would render absolute the function of his reason. If he should claim that these norms would be valid even if God did not exist, as Hugo Grotius claimed, it would mean that the Creator is placed below a product of his creation, namely human reason. The denial of God's existence and the postulation of an eternal and unchangeable natural law is only one more step.

14

For this reason Dooyeweerd rightly rejects the doctrine of Natural Law because it marks the absolutization or deification of man's logical faculties. The value of Roman Catholic Natural Law theory is that, contrary to modern views of law, it does recognize the existence of an *order* for reality as something given.

The Natural Law School absolutizes man's reason or man's social nature as the basis of certain unchanging principles of human conduct to be applied everywhere. Man's reason is thus assigned the place which rightfully can only belong to God Himself.

The directives are given by God, not created by man's reason; and man will never be able to fully fathom their magnitude. Only in so far as they touch upon life in this created world, can man, through his understanding, deduce the necessary rules for society. He discovers the norms, he does not draw them up. It is, therefore, of immense importance that man should remain conscious of the limitations and the fallibility of his intellectual functions, which are burdened by sin. This will protect him from maintaining a false pride in the products of his ingenuity, and the acknowledgement that the norms derive from principles of justice established by the Creator of heaven and earth will also safeguard him from unchecked relativism.

If then we are to speak of natural law at all, we can do so only in connection with these legal principles which are indeed independent of history, but which are not yet law, since they lack the element of positivization. Dooyeweerd will only speak of natural law as "the legal principles which must be positivized in every legal order for the simple reason that without them there can only be chaos instead of order in the life of law."[8]

Before juridical norms can become law they must be rendered positive. The acceptance of unchangeable legal rules is nothing less than an under-estimation of historicity, or the value of man as a culture forming creature. This world is subject to continuous change; new social structures emerge as for example when capitalism replaced feudalism; new views break through. These new social structures demand new legal systems. Changes in the historical situation may demand the application of new legal principles. When this is done, we do not logically deduce these from the historical givens—as the school of realism and historicism suppose—but we

15

do discover them in the meaning structure of the legal modality. Again new views call for serious and continuous reflection on the part of those who are engaged in concretizing the legal norms.

All this does not mean to say that a certain legal norm is no longer valid; it only means that at different times it requires a different formulation. Every period and every place calls for specific legal institutions, which may differ from the legal rules that may apply at other places and at other times. Only in this way can we do justice to the element of historicity, to the principle of development, which is one of the tasks of man, created in responsibility, to have dominion over the earth and to subdue it. Convincing proof of this is given by the fact that, if this requirement is not fulfilled, positive law can fall into disuse, can even become an injustice, when it is no longer the correct embodiment of a legal norm. Thus we may refer to the enormous changes which have taken place in legal rules of procedure. F. R. Bienenfeld asks in *The Recovery of Justice*:

> What could be more in contrast to the present conception of the quest for justice by procedure than the ordeals which made defeat in a duel evidence of guilt, injuries suffered in passing through fire evidence of treachery and sinking in a river an irrefutable token of innocence.[9]

The law of property and the status of women amongst primitive peoples bears no resemblance to the complicated rules of property rights and the equality of women before the law in present day Britain and America.

To be observed, legal norms must be "positivized" and they must be formed into specific, concrete legal rules, adapted to the situation of the moment. These rules are formulated by competent organs. Now it is absolutely wrong to state that this formulation should occur exclusively within the state and to say as Austin said that "the essence of law is that it is imposed upon society by a sovereign will." Such a restriction of the law to rules which are imposed by the sovereign power of the state leads to an inadmissible limitation of the notion of law. Wherever men act we meet law. That is why the law functions in every human relationship, not only political, but economic, ecclesiastical and so on. The state no doubt often establishes the most number of rules, but to argue that hence law is

16

embodied only in the rules drawn up by the state, reveals a wrong conception of law. Family, church, society and industry: they all have a law of their own. True, this law will have a different character in each of these cases, qualified as it is by the typical characteristics of the community concerned. This does not, however, detract from its legal character.

5. The Relation of Law and Morality

Legal and ethical norms are independent expressions of the created order, which in essence is *religious* not moral and they share a common basis of validity in so far as they can be traced back to the directives given by God in creation.

As we have said legal norms regulate relations between men and human institutions, in particular by means of a careful balancing of their interests. According to Dooyeweerd, in all legal phenomena we are concerned with the expression of the legal principle of "retribution," which makes these phenomena legal. Thus in public law there must be a weighing in the scales of justice of the interests of the individual and the public interest of the state. In other forms of Private Law such as torts, contract and property litigation, the interests to be balanced are between private parties. Legal norms thus bear a special relation to the external side of human relationships. Not that they are totally indifferent to motives, e.g., modern criminal law pays attention to the internal motivation of the accused, while intent plays an important part in contract and tort law. The differentiation between law and morality is one of the most difficult problems that ethics and jurisprudence are confronted with.

According to Dooyeweerd, it is incorrect to think of moral norms as being somehow autonomous and legal norms heteronomous, that is as imposed by an external authority, while morality is only binding on the individual conscience. Ethical norms have not been fixed by and for man himself in sovereign independence; they should, like legal norms, be discovered and derived from the directives given by God. Nor should we consider the law only as the "ethical minimum," since by doing so we would obliterate the distinguishing lines between the two law-spheres.

Perhaps we could broadly define the difference as follows: law

17

regulates the external relations between men, of necessity generalizing in doing so, wheras moral norms appeal to man in his individuality and bear upon his personal relationships with others. Legal norms are principles for public order, ethical norms govern men's personal lives. However, only when it is recognized that both legal and moral norms are derived from divine directives given at creation, can the danger of a threatening discrepancy between them be averted. By placing them on one common original divinely created basis we make a mutual inconsistency, as Brunner puts it in his book *The Divine Imperative*, impossible

This does not mean that at a given moment morality may not decree to break a positive legal rule. In that case, however, it must not be said that law ought to make way for morality as if law were inferior to morals, because indeed there is then something wrong with the legal rule, perhaps through over-generalization. And in that case the legal rule is not the right embodiment of the juridical norm in question.

For this reason Dooyeweerd rejects Brunner's implicit dualism between God's creation ordinances and the central divine commandment of love. For Dooyeweerd love lies at the center of the creation order and it must not be identified with the modal moment of the ethical aspect of reality. The antinomy which Brunner finds between this central divine command of love and the human legal norm of retributive justice arises from his eradication of the modal boundaries of the juridical and moral spheres.

According to Brunner, Christian ethics is the science of human conduct determined by divine action. By thus merging the ethical modality of morality with the pistical morality of faith, Brunner is led to a fundamentally erroneous definition of the relations which should exist between love and justice. For Brunner the love mentioned in the divine central commandment is absolute. It concerns the whole person and is concrete, not abstract and legal. Justice on the contrary is "general, lawful, deliberate, impersonal and objective, abstract and rational." Therefore it is a contradiction of terms to speak of a perfect justice.[10]

Dooyeweerd claims that the fundamental error of Brunner's view is here exposed. Brunner has forgotten that the fulness of the meaning of love, as revealed on Christ's Cross, is at the same time the

18

fulness of justice," he writes, "this procedure necessarily detracts from God's holiness." So far from God's love being opposed to God's justice as Brunner, Tillich and Reinhold Niebuhr all falsely suppose, it is in fact its necessary presupposition. On the Cross Christ has in principle and in fact reconciled law and love, justice and mercy, by his love vindicating God's great moral law. As our great High Priest, he paid homage to the sanctity of the moral order by himself, in his own body on the tree, paying the price of man's sinfulness and immorality. Thereby his love broke through the demands of the moral and legal order of God by satisfying its every requirement.[11]

Dooyeweerd maintains that Brunner's error is that he opposes love, as the exclusive content of the fulness of God's commandment, to the "temporal ordinances," which owing to man's fall show God's will only in a broken state. He wants to build up an ethics that will be placed solely upon the great commandment. This leads him to identify morality as such with the Christian revelation and this leads him into a complete misinterpretation of the temporal modal moral meaning of love, that is of the moral aspect of human existence. Dooyeweerd finds in this false identification due to Brunner's initial methodological distinction between the divine command of love and the creation ordinances, the reason for the antinomies which arise in his Neo-Orthodox type of Christian ethic. Brunner's conception of love as the radical opposite of justice is not really biblical at all but arises from "an absolutization of the temporal modal meaning of love." By doing so, Brunner has violated the religious dimensions of love and called in question the perfection of God's holiness and justice as revealed in Christ's death upon the Cross.

It is in terms of this profound religious understanding of God's justice and God's love as revealed in the death of His son, Jesus Christ, that we must understand Dooyeweerd's language when he writes "that retribution is the irreplaceable foundation of love in its modal moral sense." He believes that nobody can truly love his neighbor without observing the exigencies of this divine type of retribution. That is why all the moral commandments of the Decalogue make an appeal to the legal order. The commandment "Thou shalt do no murder" has no ethical meaning of love without

19

this juridical foundation in retribution. As Dooyeweerd makes clear: "Anyone who rejects the demands of retribution does harm to his neighbour in the sense condemned by the moral law of love, as it is expressed in the commandment 'Thou shalt do no murder' for he then delivers him up to injustice and violence."[12]

J. Bohatec has proved that Calvin held a similar view of the relation of justice and love. He writes: "By opposing love and justice, freedom and compulsion, the Anabaptists have forced a problem on the Reformation. Calvin does not try to get around it. Against the one-sided solution of the Anabaptists who reject the state and law, he argues that it is in the interest of love to maintain justice and the ordinances connected with it."[13]

6. Retribution, Responsibility and Freedom

Up till now the main function of the law courts in the English-speaking world has been to determine whether or not persons accused of crime committed the act in question. Such psychological considerations as motive have been taken into account only when they had a bearing on the probability or improbability of guilt or in murder cases where insanity could be pleaded. Since 1843 the law in England governing questions of criminal responsibility has been bound by the famous *McNaughten Rules* formulated by the judges of the House of Lords. According to these rules, mental abnormality sufficient to constitute a defense to a criminal charge must consist of three elements: first, the accused, at the time of his act, must have suffered from a defect of reason; secondly, this must have arisen from disease of the mind; thirdly, the result of it must have been that the accused did not know the nature of his act or that it was illegal.

In 1857, largely as a result of recommendations by the Royal Commission on Capital Punishment the law was amended in the Homicide Act which introduced the notion of "diminished responsibility." A man who is sane under the *McNaughten Rules* can, if his mental responsibility is substantially impaired, be convicted not of murder but of manslaughter.

Until recently most critics of the *McNaughten Rules* have wanted not only to retain the traditional notion that a man should not be convicted of a crime unless he is mentally responsible, but to enlarge the area within which he can plead that, by reason of some mental defect, he could not have helped doing what he did. But in the past few years some critics want to eliminate the notion of *mens rea* altogether, i.e., to throw out any idea of guilt or at least to allow it to wither away. In effect this means that we should altogether abandon the notion of punishing a man for what he knowingly and willingly did wrong and substitute a system of "social hygiene" under which conviction would be automatic once the actual crime has been proved, and the courts would then set about deciding what should be done with the criminal in the light of what was best for him and for society as a whole. In effect a big stride has already been taken in this direction, for the *Mental Health Act 1959* provides that, while a man who is sane under the *McNaughten Rules* must still indeed be convicted, the courts may order his detention for medical treatment in place of passing a penal sentence. These powers have come to be widely used. Thus in 1962 hospital orders under this Act were made in respect of 1187 convicted persons.[14]

Our only concern, say the new critics, when we have an offender to deal with, is with the future and with the rational aims of the prevention of further crime, the protection of society and if possible the cure of the offender. This revolutionary doctrine has been most powerfully advocated by Lady Wootton in two main works: *Social Science and Social Pathology* and *Crime and the Criminal Law*. Lady Wootton argues that, if the aim of the law is the prevention of socially damaging actions, the traditional doctrine which looks to the offender's culpability puts his guilty mind (*mens rea*) "in the wrong place." His state of mind should be considered not before but after conviction. One reason for this is that the line between conviction and acquittal must remain clear-cut, while any attempt to draw such a line between the normal and the abnormal is bound to fail; another is that the traditional doctrine smacks too much of the retributive theory of punishment, a theory Lady Wootton being a determinist, finds barbarous and irrational; and a third reason she gives is that, since we can never know what goes on in someone else's mind in any case, we have no possible way of discovering whether the element of "mental guilt" was present

21

or not. In short Lady Wootton wants us to abolish the doctrines of just retribution and of individual responsibility for wrongdoing and to replace these with one of treatment and cure. Punishment becomes therapeutic.[15]

At first sight it appears we have passed from the harsh and self-righteous notion of giving the wicked their just deserts to the charitable and enlightened one of tending the psychologically sick. For Lady Wootton no distinction should be drawn between criminality and sickness since the line between the sick and the healthy is irrelevant to the problems of social behavior and she is prepared accordingly to treat all offenders as "patients" and to dispense with the notions of responsibility and punishment altogether. What could be more amiable?

If we allowed individual responsibility and retribution to wither away from the criminal law, what would be lost? It may well be more than most people today realize.

The first casualty would be individual freedom. For make no mistake about it. The principle of just retribution prevents excessive severity on the one hand, and the extreme leniency on the other, in the administration of justice. If deterrence becomes the sole guiding rule in this matter, great injustices will be the result, since any "treatment" could be imposed by the government for any crime, provided it was calculated to deter others. As Professor H. L. A. Hart warns us:

> In a system in which proof of *mens rea* is no longer a necessary condition for conviction, the occasion for official interferences with our lives and for compulsion will be vastly increased. Take, for example, the notion of criminal assault. If the doctrine of *mens rea* were swept away, every blow, even if it was apparent to a policeman that it was purely accidental or merely careless and therefore not, according to the present law, a criminal assault, would be a matter for investigation under the new scheme, since the possibilities of a curable or treatable condition would have to be investigated and the condition if serious treated by medical or penal methods. . . . No one could view this kind of expansion of police powers with equanimity, for with it will come great uncertainty for the individual; official interferences with his life will be more frequent but he will be less able to predict their incidence if any incidental or careless blow may be the occasion for them.[16]

22

Once we discard the doctrines of just retribution and the individual responsibility for wrongdoing and replace these with the doctrines of determinism and treatment there will be nothing left to prevent the Home Secretary from imprisoning any citizen he dislikes for his political or religious opinions on the grounds that some expert thinks he is socially maladjusted or sick. For if crime and disease are to be regarded as the same thing, it follows that any state of mind the government chooses to call "disease" can be treated as crime and compulsorily cured.

It will be vain to plead that states of mind which displease the government need not always involve moral turpitude and do not therefore deserve forfeiture of freedom. For our new legal masters will no longer be using the concepts of desert and punishment but those of disease and cure.

According to some reformers, medical crimes are those that doctors treat and crimes that doctors treat are medical crimes. It would seem that doctors are not afraid of such tautologies. One group of doctors in America recommended the following definition for statutory use: "Mental illness shall mean an illness which so lessens the capacity of a person to use his judgement, discretion and control in the conduct of his affairs and social relations as to warrant his commitment to mental institutions."[17]

By this formula, be it noted, committal to an institution is justified by the presence of mental illness, yet this illness is itself defined only in terms of the need for committal. Under this definition wrongful detention in a mental hospital becomes impossible, inasmuch as no room is left for any criterion of health and sickness other than the fact of committal. The same committee would go even further and would revise the criminal code in such a way that no person could be convicted of any criminal charge "when at the time he committed the act with which he is charged he was suffering with mental illness, as thus defined, and in consequence thereof he committed the act." Those who determine fitness for committal by a criterion which makes their own judgment infallible would thus accordingly decide with supposed equal infallibility the question of moral responsibility. No Communist dictator could ask for greater powers over his fellow men.

By thus abolishing the notions of individual responsibility and

23

just retribution for wrongdoing social scientists are in effect lifting the criminal code out of the realm of legality altogether and placing it in the psychological, biotic and sociological realms. But crime cannot thus be reduced to psychiatric phenomena.

While psychiatry may well have its proper function to perform in criminology and penology and while we may welcome its insights into human behavior, it is exceeding its proper sphere of sovereignty when it seeks to abolish the law altogether. The law must have its own definition of legal liability, accountability and responsibility if it is to remain law. Such liability and responsibility cannot be defined by psychology or medicine. But the *legal* definition of crime and punishment may take account of the psychical, social and biological aspects of human behavior. Then in the light of such knowledge and information it can try to weigh the conflict between the interests of the accused and those of society in the scales of justice.

Then there is the moral objection that if we imprison a man in order to deter him and, through his example, others, we are using him for the benefit of society and this can only be justified if he could have helped doing what he did and thus deserved it.

When you punish a man to make of him an example to others you are using him as a means to a socially useful end: someone else's end. This, in itself would be a very wicked and cruel thing to do.

On the classical theory of punishment, which we are now being asked to reject, it was of course justified on the ground that the man deserved it. That was assumed to be established before any question of making him an example arose. You then killed two birds with one stone; in the process of giving him what he deserved you also set an example to others. But take away desert and just retribution and the whole basis of punishment or treatment disappears. Why in heaven's name should anyone be sacrificed to the good of society—unless of course they have first deserved it? Writing of this so-called Humanitarian Theory of Punishment C. S. Lewis says in *Essays on the Death Penalty*:

> This doctrine, merciful though it appears really means that each one of us, from the moment he breaks the law, is deprived of the rights of a human being. The reason is this. The humanitarian

24

theory removes from punishment the concept of desert. But the concept of desert is the only connecting link between punishment and justice. It is only as deserved or undeserved that a sentence can be just or unjust. I do not contend that the question "Is it deserved?" is the only one we can reasonably ask about a punishment. We may very properly ask whether it is likely to deter others and to reform the criminal. But neither of these last two questions is a question about justice. There is no sense in talking about a just deterrent or a just cure. We demand of a deterrent not whether it is just but whether it succeeds. Thus when we only consider what will cure him or deter others, we have tacitly removed him from the sphere of justice altogether; instead of a person, a subject of rights, we now have a mere object, a "case" to be treated in a clinic.[18]

The abolishment of *mens rea* and of individual responsibility really amounts to the depersonalization of the criminal. For the contrast between intentional, rational and deliberate actions on the one hand, and such aberrations as accident, mistake, automatism, and insanity on the other lies at the very root of our concept of what it is to be a person rather than a "mere thing." Such a view of man as a person created in God's image has in fact been derived from the biblical view of man.

By removing the notion of responsibility in deciding questions of guilt, social scientists will in effect have reduced the accused from the status of a moral subject to that of an object for medical manipulation. The scientistic theory of the cause and cure of crime inevitably has this result of depersonalization because apostate scientific doctrine is forced by its lack of a true ordering principle of science to reduce man to the level of one of his aspects, in this case his biotic, psychical and social aspects. What such modern treatment amounts to is that social scientists are demanding the full legal right to treat their criminal patients as objects for scientific experiment described for us by Dr. Edward Glover in his book *The Roots of Crime* as ranging from hypnosis, psycho-analysis, the use of wonder drugs and electric shock therapy (pp. 99-114).

For obvious reasons these methods have been kept hidden from the public and the persons who undergo such "treatment" are usually well hidden from the public gaze in graves or cells. An interesting example of such brainwashing is that of John Gates, a small business man in Clinton, Tennessee, who in 1957 attempted to

25

resist by legal action the attempt of the government to integrate his children. Gates, a healthy and vigorous man, was hauled off against his will to a nearby mental health clinic. Eight days later his emaciated dead body was delivered to his widow. According to Dr. R. P. Oliver in his article *Brainwashing in the U.S.A.*:[19] "There were blackened areas on the corpse's forehead, and the inside of the mouth was burned and charred to the depth of about one-eighth of an inch of flesh resembling the burns produced when human flesh is contacted by high voltage electricity. . . . Gates was admittedly subjected to 'electric shock therapy . . . and he died when some overtly enthusiastic social reformer turned on too much current.' " Dr. Oliver points out "There are of course other forms of 'loving care' for mental and criminal patients. A lobotomy can reduce an intelligent man to a huddled lump of living but scarcely conscious protoplasm." Such incidents have already been foretold in the prophecies of George Orwell's *1984* and David Karp's novel *ONE*. Most decent-minded people would agree that they would prefer to be punished in the old fashioned way than to be treated in this inhuman way. Even though guilty of crime, criminals are not rats and guinea pigs to be experimented upon by doctors, psychiatrists and nurses.

The so-called humanitarian and "scientistic" theory of the cause and cure of crime carries as its badge of appeal a semblance of mercy which is thus wholly false. That no doubt is why it has deceived so many church leaders in the English-speaking world.

According to C. S. Lewis, the error began with Shelley's statement that the distinction between mercy and justice was invented in the courts of tyrants. He points out that the Christian view has been "that mercy tempered justice or (on the highest level of all) that mercy and justice had met and kissed. The essential act of mercy was to pardon; and the pardon in its very essence involves the recognition of guilt and ill-desert in the recipient. If crime is only a disease which needs cure, it cannot be pardoned. How can you pardon a man for having a gumboil or a club foot?" Either he has it or he hasn't got it. Lewis concludes:

> The humanitarian theory wants simply to abolish justice and subsitute mercy for it. This means you start being kind to people before you have considered their rights, and then force upon them

supposed kindnesses which no one but you will recognize as kindnesses and which the recipient will feel as abominable cruelties. You have overshot the mark. Mercy detached from justice grows unmerciful. That is the important paradox. As there are plants which will flourish only in mountain soil, so it appears that mercy will flower only when it grows in the crannies of the rock of justice. Transplanted to the marshlands of mere humanitarianism, it becomes a man-eating weed, all the more dangerous because it is still called by the same name as the mountain variety.[20]

This humanitarian theory of mercy, in effect also has abolished the state as state. For it no longer recognizes the proper basis of human government as resting in the power of the sword (Rom. 13). It refuses to recognize that the state has been ordained by God as an instrument of common grace designed to restrain the worst consequences of human sinfulness, and that the use of power is necessary for the maintenance of justice.

The choice is plain. We can choose to retain the doctrines of just retribution and individual responsibility for wrongdoing or we can condemn ourselves to be reduced to slaves of the scientific elite. By turning our backs on God's creation order we shall discover that all defense against the exercise of arbitrary power has vanished too. If we refuse to accept God as the source of our legal norms, we shall finish up having tyrants as our masters since only God can subject power to conscience.

What we have tried to show is: (1) That "legality" cannot be absorbed by morality; (2) That "legality" cannot be absorbed by "psychology" since law has its own sovereign sphere of operation in the proper ordering of human society.

Whenever one sovereign law-sphere of God's creation attempts to infringe upon the territory of another law-sphere, antinomies always arise. Thus the antinomies of Zeno (Achilles and the tortoise, the flying arrow) are founded on the attempt to reduce the modal meaning of motion to that of space. The antinomy between retributive justice and love, to take another example, arises from the eradication of the modal boundaries of the juridical and moral spheres. The antinomy between psychological determinism and individual responsibility arises from the eradication of the modal boundaries of the psychological and juridical spheres.

All of these psychical, legal and moral aspects or spheres are genuine functions of human experience, subject to their correlative aspects of the divinely created order, interdependent, but not to be monistically reduced to each other as happens in apostate science.

Such an insight only comes to us as a result of our scripturally-normed view of reality as God's creation and not a construction of man's reason. Such a view of reality as having been created by God in principle cuts off all tendencies to absolutize a relative aspect of God's creation, e.g., psychologism, economism, biologism. Lacking a true ordering principle in the Word of God apostate social science inevitably tends towards such absolutizations of the various relative aspects of God's creation.

If scientists refuse to be taught by the Word of God what this order of God's creation is, then they will be forced to substitute some other principle of total structuration of their own devising and they will be forced to seek their ultimate principle of explanation and point of departure in one or another aspect of the created universe rather than in the Creator. As a result apostate scientists cannot grasp the intrinsic unity and coherence of all reality but are bound to fall into a false dialectical dualism in which one aspect is played over against another aspect, vitalism against mechanism in modern biology and psychological determinism over against legal responsibility in modern criminology.

7. The Enforcement of Morals in a Pluralistic Society

In recent years there has been a revival of "legal moralism," the doctrine that the public law of the state has the right, even the duty to enforce morality as such. It is a doctrine which, if it is not carefully examined, could lead to totalitarianism of the worst sort, and can only be compared with that of the Nazi regime in which the courts had the power to punish anything that was contrary to the conceptions of "sound popular feeling."

The immediate occasion which raised this important issue was itself an insignificant affair. Soon after the *Street Offences Act* became law a man named Shaw published a magazine called *Ladies' Directory* "giving the names and addresses of prostitutes, in some cases nude photographs and an indication in code of their practices." As a result he was successfully prosecuted, not only for two statu-

28

tory offenses, but for the common law crime of "conspiring to corrupt public morals." Thus the first count in the indictment alleged a conspiracy at common law to corrupt public morals, the particulars being that the defendant and the prostitutes who advertised themselves in his magazine conspired "to induce readers thereof to resort to the said advertisers for the purposes of fornication." The defense argued that there was no such general offense known to law as a conspiracy to corrupt public morals, but the House of Lords held by a majority of four to one that there was and the accused was found guilty of it. The Law lords took the opportunity in their decision to reaffirm Lord Mansfield's dictum of 1774 that "whatever is *contra bonos mores et decorum* the principles of our laws prohibit and the King's Courts, as the general censor and guardian of public morals is bound to restrain and punish."[21]

The question whether the law should have the power to restrain and punish immorality as such, that is to say without requiring proof that harm has been done was also raised by Lord Devlin in his Maccabaean Lecture delivered in 1959.[22]

Lord Devlin tells us that it was the report of the Wolfenden Committee recommending that homosexual practices between consenting adults in private should not be criminal offenses that first prompted him to undertake a theoretical examination of the relationship between morals and the criminal law. He tells us that he gave evidence before the Committee in favor of the proposed reform and that he agreed with its blunt pronouncement "that there must be a realm of private morality and immorality that is not the law's business." Then he went back to J. S. Mill's essay on Liberty for a theoretical defense of this position.

A century ago Mill, in his essay on Liberty had laid it down that "the only purpose for which power can be rightfully exercised over any member of a civilized community against his will is to prevent harm to others." Mill held that the use of the criminal law is an evil requiring justification and that it is not justified by the mere fact that the conduct which the criminal law is used to punish is an offense against the accepted moral code of the community. For the justification of punishment something more than this is required; it must be shown that the conduct punished is either directly harmful either to individuals or their liberty or jeopardizes the collective

29

interest which members of society have in the maintenance of its organization or defense. The maintenance of a given code of morals "as such" is not according to Mill, the business of the criminal law or any coercive institution. It is something which should be left to other agencies; to education, or to religion or to the outcome of free discussion among adults.

Lord Devlin tells us that since reading Mill's argument he has changed his mind. He now holds that "the suppression of vice is as much the law's business as the suppression of subversive activities," basing his argument on the premise that society has a right to protect itself and on the premise that "what makes a society is a community of ideas, not political ideas alone, but also ideas about the way its members should behave and govern their lives." Lord Devlin places many limitations on the desirability of enforcing morality. Individual liberty is valuable and its value must be thrown into the scales against the use of this general power. Such power he teaches should only be used in practice to restrain and punish conduct which meets with widespread "intolerance, indignation and disgust." Nevertheless, he leaves us in no doubt that the law has, and should have this residual power to prohibit what is immoral simply because it is immoral and to punish an immoral man simply because his immorality, deserves to be punished.[23]

This is the issue that divides Mill and his followers from their opponents. For Mill, immoral acts should never be punished for their immorality alone, but only on some other grounds such as the protection of others from harm; for Lord Devlin and James F. Stephen, immoral acts always deserve punishment, though considerations of policy may make it unwise to exact the punishment deserved.

What are Christians to think? In terms of the Christian Philosophy of Law this issue can only be successfully resolved when it is recognized that law and morality are not one but two different aspects of reality. As we have already seen, you cannot base law on morality since both are independent expressions of the created order, which is in essence religious not moral. Hence, Lord Devlin's legal moralism must be rejected since it eradicates the modal boundaries between the law aspect and the ethical aspect of God's creation. Lacking a true ordering principle in God's Word for his thought,

30

Devlin misconceives the real nature of God's creation. He accepts the Aristotelian legal philosophy which views law as part of a larger embracing whole which then is called the moral order. But, as we have seen, legal and ethical norms are not the same but different from each other. Law seeks to regulate the relations between men and human institutions by means of a careful balancing of their interests, in conformity with the social structures as given in the Creation. More specifically the public law of the state seeks to balance the various individual and social interests in the nation. Law in this sense is therefore based on the principles of the creation order but not on the principles of morality. Morality is a higher aspect of the creation order and attempts to enforce moral rules by political power inevitably result in the tyranny of the saints.

What does this mean for the law as applied by the courts and formulated by the legislature? It means that neither Parliament nor the Courts should try to make the morality of any group of citizens the legally accepted order for the nation as a whole. All that the legislature can and must do is to further "public morality," the enforcement of minimum basic standards of behavior without which society as such would collapse. The institution of the state requires, for its very existence, a basic public morality. The state must weigh in the balance of justice all of the relevant interests within the nation in order that every type of morality may find expression on the one condition that the existence of the state is not endangered and family life is protected.

Just as the state does not exist to enforce a common religious creed neither does it exist to enforce a common morality whether Christian or humanist. In advocating the right of the state to punish immorality as such Lord Devlin fails to distinguish, as Mill was careful to do, between the preservation of morality and its enforcement. Even granted that our shared morality, or part of it, ought to be preserved, it by no means follows that the machinery of the law ought to be invoked to preserve it. One might indeed go farther and claim that morality as such cannot be enforced on the grounds that to act out of fear is not to act morally. We may prohibit assault and punish an aggressor in order to prevent harm from being done; that is a proper function of the law but as Professor Hart points out:

31

Where there is no harm to be prevented and no potential victim to be protected, as is often the case where conventional sexual morality is disregarded, it is difficult to understand the assertion that conformity even if motivated merely by fear of the law's punishment, is a value worth pursuing, notwithstanding the misery and the sacrifice of freedom which it involves. The attribution of value to mere conforming behaviour, in abstraction from both motive and consequences, belongs not to morality but to taboo. This does not mean that we cannot intelligibly attribute value to lives dedicated to ideals of chastity or self-denial. Indeed the achievement of self-discipline not only in sexual matters but in other fields of conduct must on any theory of morality be a constituent of a good life. But what is valuable here is voluntary restraint, not submission to coercion, which seems quite empty of moral value.[24]

What Mill's opponents have so often failed to see is that to forego the legal enforcement of morals is by no means to adopt a laissez-faire attitude towards it; it is simply to see and accept the sometimes unattractive consequences of the fact that enforced morality is not morality at all. The refusal to distinguish sin from crime which lies at the heart of the doctrine that the law may punish immorality as such must be the death of morality itself.

Let us give an illustration. No one today believes that people must be forced to attend divine worship on the Lord's Day. At the same time the State must see to it that those who do wish to attend worship services may be allowed to do so in peace and quietness. Thus the state may justly prohibit a Sunday football match on the vacant lot next to a church while the service is being conducted. But the state may not prohibit the playing of football on Sunday as such. It may direct those interested to another vacant lot, or to another time of day. In this way the state balances a variety of individual and social interests in the nation for the sake of public welfare. The government's task is to regulate, according to the criterion of the *legal* public interest every subject's and every institution's *external* relations to the others, so that *all* individual and social relationships may flourish.

For this reason Dooyeweerd teaches that the modal moment of the juridical aspect of the state is judgment, the well-balanced harmonization of a multiplicity of interests. The public law of the state must therefore seek to maintain harmonious relationships between *all* the interests within its territory. No single interest within the borders of the state can be ignored. As Dooyeweerd says:

> The internal political activity of the State should always be guided by the idea of public social justice. It requires the harmonizing of all the interests within a national territory, in so far as they are interwoven with the requirements of the body politic as a whole. This harmonizing process should consist in weighing all the interests against each other in a retributive sense, based on the recognition of the sphere sovereignty of the various societal relationships.[25]

The purpose of government then is not to enforce morality but to protect individual and group interests against any encroachment, thus enabling them to develop in peace (I Tim. 2:3). This is what Dooyeweerd understands by the political principle of integration. Does this endow the state with the right to interfere in other social relationships and within the various spheres of society? The answer is no. The state must never interfere in the internal law and morality of the family, the school, the church, science, or industry. The internal law and morality of these social spheres is beyond the jurisdiction of the state. However, all these relationships have an external as well as internal legal function. A church, for example, is affected by a noisy factory, so that the latter is rightly prevented by law from interfering with public worship.

The state must therefore try to harmonize such external legal interests by weighing them in the balance of justice; but it must also respect the internal sphere of sovereignty of all the other sovereign social spheres. Its task is *not* to promote morality or to prohibit immorality as such but to promote justice by utilizing public law in order to maintain the *legal* order.

This Reformed type of approach implies that neither Christian morality nor any other type of morality can be legally enforced at all. Morality transcends legality in the sense that it is beyond the state's jurisdiction. Within any nation there must be *one public legal order*, but there may well be a plurality of moralities just as there are today a plurality of creeds. Only that type of morality must be prohibited which destroys this public legal order, e.g., thuggery, suttee, murder and homosexuality.

Dooyeweerd teaches that judges and legislators must be guided by the idea of justice when they deepen the life of the law in meeting new needs and solving new problems in growing societies. They should not make an absolute distinction between the idea of justice and these new situations, as if the idea of justice in law were supra-temporal. For Dooyeweerd, unlike Stammler, the idea of justice must become the connecting link between the dynamic changes within history and the supra-temporal totality of meaning centered in Jesus Christ. The idea of justice within history must become the temporal reflection not of morality but of that religious totality of meaning in the field of positive law. It must be concretized in temporal, applicable legal norms.[26]

By this means Dooyeweerd seeks to avoid the rigidity associated with the Roman Catholic doctrine of Natural Law, which does not allow for the endless variations in human situations nor for the dynamic nature of history. Legal norms can have no significance outside history. Such norms enter the process of history partly by means of the legal, moral and religious convictions of the people. These vital legal, moral and religious convictions of the people are the naive pre-theoretical intuitive experience which they have of justice and morality. It is these convictions which provide the historical basis for legislation and for the formulation of new legal rules. Good legislation demands this historical substrate and it is neglected by legislators at their peril. The most notable example that comes to mind being the attempt on the part of certain Protestant groups in America after the Great War to enforce habits of temperance upon the whole American nation by means of the Prohibition Amendment to the American Constitution. Lacking any firm basis in the consciences of the majority of Americans such a law was doomed to failure.[27]

However much judges and academics may disagree about theory, the law relating to morals will tend to reflect the popular prejudices of the time and will change as and when the prejudices change, and not before. To our Protestant ancestors the idea of two consenting adults being allowed to practice Popery even in private would have seemed utterly corrupting and subversive. So they were forbidden to do so. But when public opinion modified its prejudices, the law followed suit.

And so might the law prohibiting homosexual practices between consenting adults in private, if Sir John Wolfenden, in an effort to lend his 1957 report profundity, had not foolishly intro-

34

duced his theory into the debate which argued that such behavior should be legalized on the theoretical ground that what adults do in private is God's business, not the law's.

From the point of view of the Christian philosophy such a view is untenable. Take for example, private drinking or drug-taking. These are clearly activities which, even in excess, might be assumed to harm only the individuals concerned. So, according to Wolfenden, these activities should be none of the law's business, since the law should prohibit only actions that harm others.

But what would be the position in a society if these private activities became so prevalent as to constitute a major social problem; if so many people, for example, spent so much time drinking that production began to suffer and wives and children were deprived of food and clothing? Should not the law then regulate or control such private activities?

The answer, of course, is that it is almost impossible, in an organized society, to conceive of a private act which might not, in some circumstances harm others in one way or another. Just as low standards in personal hygiene can endanger public health, so low standards in private morals can endanger public welfare. It would seem therefore wholly misleading to try to draw any theoretical line beyond which the law may not trespass. All human activity, however private, can legitimately be the law's business, whenever it disturbs the public order and interest.

The state, that is to say, must be allowed to regulate morality from the standpoint of the public order and interest. And this may require the regulation rather than the prohibition of such evils as gambling, prostitution and nudism. Thus, for example, public order today requires that nudes cannot be allowed to flock around our cities. The solution then should be to limit them to nudist camps. This does not mean that Christians have to approve such conduct. As Paul well says in this respect:

> We all know that the law is an excellent thing, provided we treat it as law, recognizing that it is not aimed at good citizens, but at the lawless and unruly, the impious and sinful, the irreligious and worldly, at parricides and matricides, murderers and fornicators, perverts, kidnappers, liars, perjurers (I Tim. 1:8-10).

In his common grace and forbearance the Lord God has

ordained coercive government over men precisely on account of their sinfulness as a method of restraining the worst consequences of sin. The state exists to punish evildoers rather than to cure them or reform them (Rom. 13).

8. *The Reformed Approach to the Problem of Homosexuality*

It is claimed by those seeking to reform the present law under which male homosexuals are now punished in both Britain and America that those who resist such reform are lacking in Christian compassion because homosexuals are born with their affliction and should not therefore be punished for it.

As we consider this matter as Reformed Christians we need always to remember the words of our Savior to those who dragged before him the woman taken in adultery, "He that is without sin among you, let him first cast a stone at her" (John 8:7). In this matter we can none of us argue from a position of moral superiority. The person who reckons that he can, has never seen the darkness of his own heart or understood his real position before God without the saving cleansing grace of Christ in his life. As Paul says we have all sinned and come short of the glory of God, and if our sin has taken another form than homosexuality are we the better persons for that? Of course not. Sin is sin no matter what form it takes, and we should not fall into the Roman Catholic error of classifying some sins as being less grievous than others, and therefore of less consequence. Whenever we think of the problem of homosexuality, as Reformed Christians we must say "There but for the grace of God go I," and say it with true humility and thankfulness and not in a spirit of superiority.

Further we need to remember that to a large extent we all carry some share of blame for the sinful acts of others. Obviously each man is individually accountable for his own conduct, but there is a very real sense in which we have a responsibility for the sins other people commit. This has been true from the beginning. Adam and Eve started a chain reaction called original sin which has been going on ever since, and which the grace of God alone can break. Thus the vicious, and perhaps untrue, defamation of another's character may lead to a person's suicide. The irresponsible behavior of parents has bred many children who became dangerous criminals. None of us is "an island unto himself" living in a social vacuum, and whatever we do or say will have its effect for good or ill on those around us.

This surely means that the state has a collective responsibility to legislate in such a way that it will deter people from corrupting weaker minded persons and will clearly indicate that it intends to protect the young and the innocent from exploitation by adults. It is here that the proposed reform of the law concerning homosexuals goes astray. The ordinary person in the street is bound to assume if the law is changed to legalize homosexual acts between adult consenting males that such behavior has been made *morally* as well as *legally* acceptable.

The question must be asked whether the present case for reform is well based, whether homosexuals are properly to be regarded as a persecuted minority group. To say that they are is to ask for more than an end to the legal punisment of homosexual practice; it is to demand its social acceptance.

This is something that Wolfenden assumed would not and could not happen; an assumption that was part of his premise, namely that the law has no business interfering with sin as such or trying to enforce private sexual morality by means of penal sanctions. Yet there seems little doubt that the demand for the social acceptance of homosexuality will gather momentum if the Wolfenden proposals become law. If it eventually succeeds, we shall have a society in which homosexual relationships are considered no less "natural" or more shameful than heterosexual relationships.

Homosexual couples will be free to embrace in public without risk of causing offense; homosexual love stories will be fittingly told on the stage. It may be that the theme of homosexual literature, which at the moment is "pity us" will change to "envy us." Likewise homosexual couples will be free to "get married" and set up a home. Do the heterosexual advocates of reform look forward to having such homosexual couples living next door to them as neighbors? Will the state recognize such marriages and, if so, will it also permit legal divorce for such couples? In a sense, after all, it is the heterosexual majority, subject to divorce laws and civil penalties for adultery, which will be discriminated against, once the homosexual minority has won the total freedom it seeks.

Do the ecclesiastical advocates of reform fully realize that when homosexual practice ceases to be a crime it will also cease to be stigmatized as a sin, or that the case for the one makes the other inevitable?

At present their voices seem muted, because they evidently share the illusion that the Wolfenden report leaves nothing to be desired except its enactment. But, if they were to examine the report anew, they might find that it neither provides sufficiently convincing or relevant reasons for holding a moral line nor offers any real protection against such a line being breached. It is time that Christian leaders in America and Britain sounded the warning before it is too late and our societies take the fateful step into complete moral decadence.

If the proposed reform is carried through, it will become legal for a man over the age of 21 to sell his body in the same way as a female prostitute does. If this happens the new legislation will not only open the way for a vast increase in homosexual behavior but also greatly increase the spread of venereal diseases since these can be passed on by males as well as females. Far from helping those who have homosexual tendencies, such a change in the law will only serve to provide them with even greater temptation and thus plunge them still deeper in their sin.

Whatever the liberal modernist theologians teach, homosexuality *is* a sin. Even while we act with compassion we must remember what God's Word has to say about this, because it is only when we recognize that homosexual behavior is a sin and not merely a psychological aberration, that we shall be in a position to help. In the Scriptures, we find the prohibition or categoric condemnation of homosexual practices in Leviticus 18:22 and 20:13; Romans 1:22; I Corinthians 6:9-11; I Timothy 1:10. This biblical witness is documented by Bailey in his contribution to *Homosexuality and the Western Christian Tradition*. By comparison with the mass of material drawn from ecclesiastical and other history which is found in this book, the part given to biblical texts is extremely small. Bailey thinks that the prejudice dominating the Church on the subject of homosexuality derives from a faulty exegesis of the

38

story of Sodom (Gen. 18), namely that the Lord will punish with a terrible extermination those who commit such crimes. He thinks that this is a faulty interpretation on the grounds that it is impossible to prove that it was a case of homosexual offenses. The Hebrew "*yada*" does not always designate sexual "knowledge" and the Sodomites only wished to "make the acquaintance" of strangers. But Bailey does not explain how such conduct could constitute a violation of hospitality which entailed their total destruction, nor why Lot tried to avoid the thing to the point of offering up his daughters to their violence.

With regard to the indisputable condemnation of homosexual practices in Leviticus 18:22 and 20:13, it is explained away by liberal theologians that these texts are not strictly speaking a prohibition of homosexual practices as such, but the prohibition of relations with foreign cults, of which the religious prostitution of men was an integral part. It was not, then, a question of moral purity, but of purity of creed. Writing of these texts Bailey says: "There is hardly any reason to agree that vices against nature were customary among the Egyptians and the Canaanites, there is none to confirm that these had any place in their forms of worship."[28]

As for the judgment in the New Testament, Bailey finds it "very clear."[29] In his monograph, Bailey covers in two and a half pages the most decisive texts of the New Testament with the purpose of investigating if the Greek descriptions of homosexuals are correctly rendered in the English translation. He gives no exegesis.

The liberal modernist result of studying the New Testament declarations on the subject come to the conclusion that Jesus does not condemn homosexuality and Paul only envisages the excess of ancient society, without touching on the problem of homosexuality as an "innate tendency," as it presents itself to us today. Such a view of homosexuality as an "innate tendency" tends to put all theological judgment on the wrong foot from the start, reducing it to silence. If it is indeed true that homosexuality is an innate tendency with which one is born then obviously morality does not enter the question since it can neither be pardoned nor condoned. The Conference of Boldern has shown just how arguable this theory of innate tendency is.

As far as the differentiation of homosexuality is concerned, the

39

distinction drawn by the British Medical Association seems more just. It distinguishes between "idiopathic" (inborn) homosexuality and "acquired" homosexuality; the first describing subjects who from the earliest age have felt attracted by their own sex. This is an extremely small percentage of men, about 4% of homosexuals. Balancing them are the very large numbers who practice both homosexual and heterosexual behavior, and who have come to their perverse practices by seduction. It is the rapid increase of this type which is causing the problem today in public life and which involves the responsibility of every Christian citizen.[30]

The doctrine of the innate tendency further provides homosexuals with the ready-made excuse that they cannot help what they are doing because they have been born with it. Those who have been afflicted at birth with this failing should therefore not be held responsible for their behavior on the ethical plane.

Having declared the biblical criterion irrelevant and accepting the doctrine of the "innate tendency" the moralists of the new legality then insist that we approach the homosexual in his different nature with a "much greater understanding" and spare him all blame for his conduct.

From this point on no notice need any longer be taken of the crucial distinction between homosexual *tendency* and *practice*, a distinction which alone gives a meaning to the biblical condemnation of the practice rather than the tendency towards homosexuality. This proceeding is justified by the argument that we must seek to understand rather than condemn the homosexual and seek to cure him rather than punish him.

If homosexuality is indeed a disease requiring treatment rather than punishment, surely the same criterion applicable to other infectious diseases should also apply. At present anyone found contaminated by an infectious disease is required by law to undergo medical treatment and to be secluded from society.

By the same token why then do not the advocates of the new legality demand of the state that the dread disease of homosexuality (if such it is) be treated by doctors and that the homosexual be quarantined until he is cured? We do not allow people with typhoid to roam our streets.

Whether we look upon the homosexual as sick or sinful it would

40

seem that both schools of thought require his seclusion from healthy society until such time that he be restored to normal heterosexuality.

In any case we must ask, if it is right to discard the biblical norm in the name of pity. Anyone who studies the sixth chapter of I Corinthians without prejudice must conclude on this point that both the accusing law and the act of salvation accomplished by Christ and the gift of the Holy Spirit are equally in the eyes of the New Testament the very working of God's mercy towards mankind, while the position under attack belittles both the law of God and the Gospel of grace.

The theory of the inherency (innateness) of homosexuality has been exhaustively exposed by the English sociologist Richard Hauser in his book *The Homosexual Society*. Using as the basis for his researches the results of numerous interviews with and between homosexuals, Hauser has formulated a doctrine of the homosexual type which describes homosexual behavior with great analytical objectivity.

Hauser's researches have led him to the conclusion that the great majority of homosexuals are ambivalent and he finds the line between the normal and the abnormal extremely fine. He suggests that the risk of crossing this line is greatest during adolescence when the young man passes through a phase of "ambivalent" sexuality and it is the arresting of emotional and social development which tends to produce the homosexual tendency. Fundamentally homosexuality is a stress problem due to deprivation or distress from failure to adjust with one's social environment. This prevents the individual from attaining his full emotional and social development. Hauser explains homosexuality as a method of escape from the realities of life. This is why, like alcoholism, homosexuality is not a *cause* but a *consequence* of social tension such as the break up of home life. For these reasons it is necessary to oppose the widespread view that this fixation is inherent in the homosexual deviate. As Hauser says "We have tried to expose the spectre of inherent homosexuality and to show that the homosexual way of life has social causes."[31]

The great value of Hauser's study lies in the fact that it dispels the fog which has accumulated around the discussion of the thesis of the inherent or innate homosexual. Hauser has proved that the real problem does not consist so much of people who are born with homosexual tendencies but in a growing number of "bi-sexual"

41

types who have slipped into homosexual behavior. They constitute today an aggressive "social infection" which menaces all our youth. Faced with this grave social danger, it is imperative that we do not allow our preconceived theories to hide from us the facts of the problem before us.[32]

In discussing the grounds of the appearance of the homosexual tendency, we must try to hold on to that which can be proved by strict analysis and not be swayed by our own prejudices. If research proves that "the homosexual is made rather than born as such" then we must seek to discover the causes of his deviation. Has it been brought about by social stress or has it been acquired from others by infection?

Hauser's researches show clearly that the majority of practicing homosexuals exhibit not only a behavior pattern, but a mentality which cannot escape the judgment of biblical morality. In innumerable conversations with homosexuals, Hauser heard them say that their life is quite preoccupied with parties, pleasure seeking, amusements, "kicks." There is nothing they hate more than the conventional boring life, the daily routine of the wretched family man who wears himself out with material cares about his family. Often they declare bluntly "I wouldn't want to be tied down";[33] "I've no wish to care about other people, I want to live my own life." The role of the family man is rejected. Throughout their statements show that they are only interested in themselves and they are fascinated by sex.[34] Besides, there is that characteristic amorality which was not overlooked by the defecting diplomats Burgess and Maclean. This amorality creates a strange climate beyond good and evil which thinks nothing of betraying one's nation's secrets to the enemy to further the gratification of one's lusts.[35]

It is impossible that this worship of sex and this refusal to accept family responsibilities should not come under the influence of a moral judgment, since, according to the biblical criterion, it is not only glaring crimes that incur this judgment.

While condemning the actual practice, however, the law must not only deter, restrain and try to prevent such men from exploiting the weakness of others, it must also seek the help of the Church in trying to cure homosexuality.

For the theologians Bailey and Thielicke such a cure is considered to be impossible since they hold to the theory of the "innate" character of homosexuality. Fortunately a growing number of psychiatrists as well as the sociologist Hauser believe that homosexuality can be cured. "You should have seen the joy and relief felt by those who find that they will not always have to remain in this state."[36]

Of all people the Christian should be able to hold out the hope of a cure to this heart-breaking fixation, when he reads from Paul's pen that men who were once of this type were a part of the Church at Corinth. Now, their impious practices belong henceforth irrevocably to the past for—and note the triple contrast—"ye are washed, ye are sanctified, ye are justified in the name of the Lord Jesus, and by the Spirit of our God" (I Cor. 6:11).

Only the Gospel of God can truly effect a cure for this evil. And it is our responsibility as Christians to see that this is made plain. Here is where we have failed. The Church on the whole has ignored the homosexual and his need for the Gospel. We have fought shy of what is a nasty subject. The respectable ears of our congregations do not want to be shocked by hearing of the mental and spiritual agony of a sizeable proportion of their fellow men.

Every Christian has a responsibility to these men to tell of the Christ Who can save, of the God Who shows mercy to the repentant sinner, and of the Holy Spirit who can deliver them from the bondage of sin. This is the work we must do, and it is perhaps because of our failures to do this that the initiative to help these men has come in another way from apostate psychiatrists and sociologists. For this reason we need Christian rehabilitation centers where Christian doctors and clergy can work together in helping these men. It is with gratitude that we take note of the conviction expressed by many such Christian doctors and psychiatrists that, by an encounter with the redeeming power of Jesus Christ, a radical change in the situation is possible. They bear out their conviction with a great number of individual stories. Thus a report of the British Medical Association describes, in a paragraph on "Conversion and the Homosexual" changes which have occurred in cases of homosexuality acquired later in life.[37]

43

In these accounts of cures two significant elements constantly appear:

(1) The expendability of the man, who devotes himself to the service of a higher cause. In the life of the individual the realization of the Lordship of Christ takes on a new meaning, giving him a goal which dominates him in the place of the aimlessness and introversion which had previously disintegrated his soul. The thing that the Prior of The Little Brothers of Jesus describes in the letters to his Order can be seen happening "chastity becomes possible as the manifestation of a total surrender to Jesus of Nazareth."[38]

(2) The necessity for a Christian community. Constantly, renewal begins in the life of homosexuals by means of a Christian group "which creates for him and around him a new moral climate"[39] by putting before him the goal which we have just mentioned. Naturally, a group for whom the mission of showing forth the lordship of God has become the specific aim can communicate this same objectivity to the homosexual.

Any cure in the Christian sense begins by asking the question: "Do you want to be saved?" Here this question takes on a decisive value.[40]

From this point on, the path of renewal will be marked out by positive steps; looking back at the past and acknowledging sinful behavior, confession, acceptance of forgiveness, beginning of the fight against lustful impulse, and living constantly in Christ under the guidance of the Holy Spirit.[41] The thing that Paul describes in I Corinthians 6:11 is an experience found at the end of all moral instruction, as at the beginning. Without a new creation in Christ, it is not possible for Christian moral teaching to prove effective.

Concluding this discussion, it must be pointed out that the Christian community today should defend itself from becoming deprived of its own distinctive biblical moral criteria and from a relativization of its judgment in which the Old and New Testament have no longer any relevance. Addressing the Fifth International Reformed Congress the Rev. Dr. P. Ch. Marcel spoke of this devaluation of Christian morality as follows:

> Today there is taking place a devaluation of the moral principles of the Bible as well as the denial of the regeneration and power of the Holy Spirit. We observe a conformity of the teaching of the

44

Church to the world, and to unregenerate public opinion. The theologians have become the "idealogians" of the spirit of their time; they express the ideas of their time and provide them with a theoretical justification. What makes it so serious is that this happens precisely in the Church, in the name of Christianity and its future, in the name of love and understanding for men. The theologians work not to christianize humanity but to harmonize Christendom. If the world is present in the Church, how then will the Church be present in the world? . . . With a mediocre God, a mediocre Christ, a mediocre revelation, a mediocre morality, will the Church no more have a mission of grandeur? Christianity without the Cross—can it bring something to the world?[42]

Marcel then points out that:

The new ethic is not different from the old paganism; it is an atheism under the mask of Christianity, a dissolution of the Christian morality under the color of piety. . . . In reality people now live without God, without his norms and his power. God appears only at the end of the line of concession and compromise; his part is only to overlook man's mistakes and weaknesses. The belief in the renewal of man also has been devaluated and destroyed.[42]

The biblical judgments regarding homosexuality are exactly appropriate because they touch on homosexual behavior, the actual practice rather than the tendency. And it is this, in fact which constitutes the problem today. It is impossible to see how the rule of God's sovereignty should not be valid and salutary for the problem of homosexuality as it is for all other cases of human sinfulness and deviation. In I Corinthians chapter six, Paul has said typical and definitive things, describing the *norm* as well as the *power* of the new life in Christ.

The significance of this for the Christian community as far as homosexuality is concerned has been well expressed in the final report of the Commission of Social Studies of the Swiss Pastoral Society meeting on September 2, 1963:

The community on the one hand and Christians on the other have to witness before the homosexuals, their brothers, before those who suffer deeply from their constitution, that God's mercy is just as necessary and just as effective for them as for all other weak and sinful men.[43]

Our analysis has we hope showed the need to think of the

Christian ethic as applying to individuals, including homosexuals, as well as to society as a whole. In its particular principles, the redemption of humanity achieved in Christ, the expectation of his total and visible lordship, and the mission of making Christ's sovereignty real over all aspects of life, this ethic must discern the criteria which condition it. As soon as we become aware of these principles, there can be no question of compromise in this world for the Christian ethic, a sort of recognition of eros and libido as independent values, as some advocates of the new morality now demand. For these men there can no longer be any question of divine commandments from above or of absolute precepts. Modern man they tell us needs a modern ethic, one that takes into account "individual needs and particular situations," and defines "what in reason could be asked of him." Thus H. A. Williams writes in his contribution to the Cambridge symposium *Soundings* that Freud's discoveries may have made necessary "a reassessment of moral values."

> Where the reassessment is necessary is in our understanding of how and when we give ourselves and how and when we refuse to do so. This makes it impossible to describe certain actions as wicked and others as good. For only I myself can discover in what actions I am giving myself and in what actions I am refusing to give. . . . A great deal of what Christians often call virtue, on closer inspection turns out to be cowardice—a refusal to give myself away because I am too frightened to do it.[44]

Williams then gives as an example of what he means the self-giving of the prostitute in the Greek film "Never on a Sunday" by means of which the sailor with whom she had intercourse "acquires confidence and self-respect. He goes away a deeper fuller person than when he came in. What is seen is an act of charity which proclaims the glory of God. The man is now equipped as he was not before."[42]

What Williams has forgotten is that it is the lordship of Christ which is the decisive criterion of the Christian ethic, and on this point, the task of the Christian sexual ethic in its entirety consists of a submission and control of natural tendencies rather than of their expression in the interests of self-awareness or self-gratification.

It is difficult, if not impossible, to discover any point of contact between the teaching of this new morality and the teaching of Christ.

46

Our Lord often had dealings with people whose lives were morally disordered. He showed them remarkable understanding and compassion, but we never find him characterizing their conduct as otherwise than sinful. Thus to the woman taken in adultery he said "Go, and sin no more" (John 8:11).

Far from encouraging the abandonment of all rules, all his utterances on sexual morality presuppose the Old Testament code, with its concern for the strict regulation of behavior between the sexes. Our Lord's ethic was one of perfection and He invites us not to discard but to go one better than the Jewish Law.

Christ was fully as aware as any modern psychologist of the pervasive sexuality of human nature. But his teaching was that we should be pure, not merely an external act, but interior thought as well.

The so-called reformers draw a contrast between chastity and charity, arguing that their "situational ethic" allows more perfect scope for the latter. But surely just the opposite is the case.

If charity has any meaning at all, it stands for the profound love or reverence which one human person has for another and in virtue of which they treat each other as ends, not as means.

The whole point of the Christian sex ethic is that only marriage provides a setting where this is possible. All other relationships are transient and casual; there is no giving of one to the other without reserve and an element of selfishness and mutual exploitation is always present.

If reserved for marriage, however, the precious gift of sex is hallowed in a context of mutual obligation in the sight of God and man, of absolute and unreserved surrender of the one to the other, and of family life.

True love is never free. It entails sacrifice, adjustment, cooperation and responsibility for the happiness of another human being. Fornication is a gross sin because at its deepest level it is an example of pure physical selfishness and greed. To the invariable excuse given for adultery and extra-marital relationships, "We are in love," let the Christian answer, "What you really mean is that you need each other sexually." There is a tremendous difference between sex experienced within monogamous marriage and so-called free love either heterosexual or homosexual. If we are truly in love we shall wait for the fulness of self-giving only possible within marriage. Because love is priceless we pay a higher price for love than for any other of God's gifts.

The new morality works with a conception of man in which sexual satisfaction has become an absolute value in itself needing no higher justification. This is the ultimate logic of the new morality and this is why every true Christian must oppose it, since for the true Christian, man is a spiritual being, whose destiny is fellowship with God. Everything in his life must therefore be subordinated to this end. This applies, particularly to the sex instinct, for unless it is brought into subjection to Christ it can effectively hide the vision of God from us. For this reason the writer agrees with some profound words of Klaus Bockmuhl written in *La Revue Réformée*:

> Faced with the campaign to rehabilitate homosexuality within the Christian ethic, we will have to give the same answer with which we will oppose those other similar attempts we see today, and which present the same kind of arguments, trying to "modernize" the Christian sexual ethic. . . . The present attempts now being made, on the plane of homosexuality, to arrive at a fundamental modification of the Christian judgment are in the end nothing more than a particular episode of the vast offensive which has set itself up with a view to transforming *theology into anthropology*. We see this in the attempt to neutralize the biblical testimony, in the disdain (of modern theologians) for the Apostle Paul and in the elimination of the doctrine of the justification of the sinner. It is no longer a question of accusation and justification, of death and resurrection with Christ. . . .
>
> In any case, the indications are multiplying of an attempt once again to reduce not only dogmatics, but also theological ethics to (apostate) anthropology. And, once more, a generation will find itself faced with the necessity of choosing whom it wishes to serve.[45]

The advocates of the new morality view orthodox Christian morality as an irrational prejudice which infringes on human freedom and which denies proper recognition to one's fellow human beings. Instead of viewing homosexuality as unnatural and sinful the "reformers" now teach that it is no more unnatural than eating cooked meat or wearing clothes.[46]

The orthodox Christian detects the following apostate principles at work in the arguments for introducing the "new legality." (1) Because the apostate humanist thinks that God is dead or does not exist, he argues that all kinds of behavior are now permissible including sexual intercourse between men. (2) Because the apostate humanists imagine that man rather than God is now sovereign ruler of the world, and therefore the rightful source of his own standards and values, they argue that man must not be forced into obeying the Ten Commandments or the moral teachings of Jesus Christ. (3) According to these apostate humanists man does not need to be converted and cleansed of his sinfulness as the Bible teaches, instead modern man must be recognized in his humanistic faith in his own power and science, and Christians must be educated into recognizing the non-Christian's right to do as he pleases. (4) These unbelievers further believe that the law of the state must serve all man's desires, passions and lusts and that modern man no longer needs to be disciplined or restrained by God's Law revealed in the Bible. Their slogan is "No God, therefore no master over us," and therefore they further teach that modern men need no longer live *under* the law but *over* it. (5) Finally the advocates of this new godless legality believe that the established religion of the community must become that of "scientific" humanism rather than Christianity. A common faith in man's capacity to save himself by his own reason, planning and science must replace the old faith of America, Britain and Canada that Jesus Christ alone is God's appointed means of salvation.

This legal and moral nihilism has become a deadly menace not only to the state but to society as a whole attacking our nations at their vital moral and religious roots and threatening to overturn God's legal and moral order for man.

For this reason Christians must oppose the present attempt to legalize homosexuality. It is not only contrary to God's declared law but it will be a change for the worse, not only in terms of the moral standing of our nations as a whole, but also it will hinder rather than help the individual homosexual. The proposed change thus reveals itself to be the very antithesis of the compassion it is supposed to represent.

Conclusion

Let all true lovers of freedom under God's law be warned in time. The substitution of the new morality and the new legality for the Christian morality and legality as the basis of America's

49

and Britain's and Canada's legal and political system will involve nothing less than a revolution in the existing structure of our Anglo-American-Canadian law and it will pave the way for the totalitarian enslavement of the American and British peoples by apostate social planners and scientists.

A sobering picture of the logical end-product of the new morality and the new legality is given by C. H. and Winifred Whiteley in their recent book *The Permissive Morality*. The Whiteleys, both of whom teach philosophy at Birmingham University, England, write as scholars who "believe that a man without religious faith lacks one important incentive to moral conduct." After a careful analysis of present trends they picture "the fully developed Permissive Society in which individual choice is replaced by social conditioning":

> We can imagine that in such a society the issue between chastity and sexual freedom would be settled in favour of freedom, premarital sexual experience would be normal, adultery a triviality, and a change of partner no more serious than a change of job. The logical outcome might well be the disappearance of marriage save between those who positively desired children and as much family life as the new society would allow. Fresh techniques of contraception would limit parenthood to the genuine enthusiasts, and with the development of eugenics even these might find themselves submitted to a screening procss before they were permitted to breed. . . .
> A socity of the utmost blandness would ensue. . . . Training, job, meals, living quarters, medical attention and recreation would be provided by a single public organization so that the ordinary fellow need not worry about these things but could give all his attention when off duty to amusing himself. Advertising would be easily transformed into state propaganda. Individual protest would be ignored unless it became persistent, when it would be treated as symptomatic of an illness to be cured at public expense. If a man proved a reliable worker and amenable only when under the influence of drugs, then drugged he would be. Training-in of suitable attitudes would be undertaken at school and later on the job.
> All this is the logical outcome of the morally permissive trend; if the ordinary person is to be relieved of responsibility, some few persons in authority must undertake it on his behalf. Thus the need for individual conscience and individual moral struggle would disappear. And so the managements' idea of the greatest happiness of the greatest number could be economically dispensed through the community.[47]

50

Thus will God punish us for attempting to overthrow the legal and moral order of His universe. We can choose to be governed by God and to live under His law or we can condemn ourselves to be ruled by the new scientific "elite." Without a firm belief in God's moral and legal ordering of man's world there can be no valid ground or basis for the enforcement of law and order in society. When God and His laws and creation structures are rejected by nations then all defense against arbitrary power vanishes too at the same time. If Americans and Britons refuse to acknowledge God as their ultimate sovereign in this life they will finish up having tyrants as their masters because it is only God Himself who can subject the powers of politicians, judges, police and scientists to conscience. Without such a conscience enlightened by God's Word and God's Law there can be no abiding defense against injustice and tyranny.

It is therefore imperative that Christians realize the vital necessity for a constant witness on their part to the saving reforming and liberating power of the Lord Jesus Christ. Before they can hope to change the moral and legal direction now being taken by the nations of the English-speaking world they must reverse the present apostate religious direction. The Christian philosophy of life must not be allowed to hang in thin air but it must be brought down to earth in the hearts and consciences of the common people and in the concrete political, economic and legal situations of life.

Let Christians everywhere set about creating an informed Christian public opinion by establishing their own day schools, universities, newspapers, radio and television networks. It is stupid to bemoan the absence of a specifically biblical approach to law and politics when we have done next to nothing to create an informed Christian public opinion.

The problem of enforcing morals cannot be discussed only as one of jurisprudence. To do so merely clouds the issue. Until our Anglo-American-Canadian societies evolve a new Christian consensus about morality, the lawyers can be of little help. If the protracted controversy started by the *Wolfenden Report* has done nothing else, it has made this truth crystal clear.

Our generation is now faced with the necessity of choosing

51

which god it wishes to serve, and it must realize what fateful moral and legal consequences hang upon that choice.

As we have seen life is religion. It is not morality nor is it science. Life is religion and the service of the one true God whom Christ revealed or of a false god and idol of man's own devising.

For this reason Christians must first work to bring about a religious change in men's hearts before they can hope to persuade them to adopt Christian moral and legal standards. It is impossible to enforce such Christian standards upon people whose religious foundations have been shattered. Hence Christians must with God's help seek to rebuild the foundations of their nations upon a truly biblical basis which alone can truly reconstruct the legal and political order.

SCHEME OF DOOYEWEERD'S COSMOLOGY

Succession of Spheres	Modal Moment	Order of Time	Science
1. The numerical	Discrete quantity	Succession and relation of numbers	Mathematics
2. The spatial	Extension	Spatial simultaneity	Mathematics
3. The physical	Movement	Measured time according to the movement of the earth around its axis	Physics and Chemistry
4. The biological	Organic Life	Organic development	Biology, Physiology, Morphology
5. The psychical	Feeling and Sensation	Succession of Feelings	Empirical Phychology
6. The analytical	Theoretical Distinction	Logical prior and posterior	Logic
7. The historical	The cultural process of development of human society	Historical development in the sense of periodicy	History
8. The linguistic	Symbolic signification	Pauses, tenses, declensions, etc.	Philology, Semantics
9. The social	Social intercourse	Social status and convention	Sociology
10. The economic	Economy	Calculation of interest, investments, etc.	Economics
11. The aesthetic	Harmony	Unity of time, aesthetic duration	Aesthetics
12. The juridical	Retribution	The course of retribution, expiring of contracts, etc.	Jurisprudence
13. The ethical	Love of one's neighbor	Prudence	Ethics
14. The faith or pistical	Transcendent certainty regarding the origin	The reference to eternity	Theology

Dooyeweerd does not consider this scheme as final, since further research may reveal more modal spheres or may cause some change in the order of the spheres.

53

REFERENCES AND NOTES

1 Norman St. John-Stevas, *Life, Death and the Law*. A study of the relationship between law and Christian morals in the English and American legal systems (Eyre and Spottiswoode, London, 1960), p. 350. Cf. Glandville Williams, *The Sanctity of Life and the Criminal Law* (Faber & Faber, London, 1958), and A. L. Goodhart, *English Law & Moral Law*.

2 David Knowles, *The Evolution of Medieval Thought* (Longmans, London, 1962), p. 257.

3 A. P. D'Entreves, *Aquinas; Selected Political Writings* (Blackwell, Oxford, 1948), p. xiii of introduction.

4 A. P. D'Entreves, *Natural Law* (Hutchinson, London, 1957), p. 42.

5 August Lang, "The Reformation and Natural Law" in the book *Calvin and the Reformation* (Revell, Chicago, 1909), p. 94ff.

6 Herman Dooyeweerd, *A New Critique of Theoretical Thought* (Presbyterian and Reformed Publishing Co., Philadelphia, 1953), Vol. 1, p. 28.

7 Herman Dooyeweerd, *ibid.*, p. 102.

8 Herman Dooyeweerd, *Encl. Jurisprudence* (Amsterdam, 1949), Vol. II, p. 158.

9 F. R. Bienenfeld, *Rediscovery of Justice* (Allen & Unwin, London), p. 4.

10 Emil Brunner, *The Divine Imperative* (Lutterworth, London, 1949), p. 450. Cf. Brunner's different teaching in *Justice and the Social Order* (London, 1945).

11 E. L. H. Taylor, The Death of the Lord, *HIS DOMINION* (Bracebridge, Canada), May 1, 1961, and *Australian Church Quarterly*, Jan. 1962.

12 Herman Dooyeweerd, *A New Critique*, Vol. 11, p. 161.

13 J. Bohatec, *ibid.*, as quoted by Dooyeweerd, p. 161.

14 *Criminal Statistics*, London, 1962, p. 94.

15 Barbara Wootton, *Social Science and Social Pathology* (Allen & Unwin, London, 1959), chapter 8. Mental Disorder and the Problem of Moral and Criminal Responsibility. Also *Crime and the Criminal Law* (London, 1963).

16 H. L. A. Hart, *The Morality of the Criminal Law* (Oxford, 1965), p. 26.

17 Quoted by Barbara Wootton in *Social Science and Social Pathology*, p. 244, who subjects it to a devastating criticism.

18 C. S. Lewis, "The Humanitarian Theory of Punishment," as published in *Essays on the Death Penalty* (St. Thomas Press, Houston, P. O. Box 35096, Houston 35, Texas), p. 3.

19 R. P. Oliver, *Brainwashing in the U.S.A.* (American Opinion, Belmont, Mass. 02178, U.S.A.). Cf. David Karp, *One* (Gollancz, London, 1954).

20 C. S. Lewis, *ibid.*, p. 11ff.

21 Patrick Devlin, *The Enforcement of Morals* (Oxford, 1965), p. 88.

22 *Ibid.*, Morals and the Criminal Law, p. 1ff.

23 *Ibid.*, 13ff. and 102ff. For J. S. Mill's essay on *Liberty* consult edition by R. B. McCallum (Blackwell, Oxford, 1946).

24 H. L. A. Hart, *Law, Liberty and Morality* (Oxford, 1963), p. 80.

[25] Herman Dooyeweerd, *A New Critique*, Vol. III, p. 446.
[26] Herman Dooyeweerd, *Encyclopedia of Jurisprudence*, Vol. II, p. 127.
[27] Robert M. Miller, *American Protestantism and Social Issues, 1919-1939* (Oxford, 1959).
[28] D. S. Bailey, *Homosexuality and the Western Christian Tradition* (London, 1955), p. 69.
[29] *Ibid.*, p. 70
[30] Richard Hauser, *The Homosexual Society* (London, 1962), p. 78.
[31] *Ibid.*, p. 9. See also R. J. Rushdoony, *The Religion of Revolution.*
[32] *Ibid.*, p. 144.
[33] *Ibid.*, p. 86.
[34] *Ibid.*, pp. 55, 72, 79, 89.
[35] A. Pudry and D. Sutherland, *Burgess and McLean* (London, 1963) p. 52.
[36] Hauser, *op. cit.*, p. 20. Also M. Zeegers, *Der Homosexualle Nachste*, p. 162.
[37] *Homosexuality and Prostitution.* A Memorandum of Evidence prepared by a special committee of the Council of the British Medical Association, London, December, 1955, pp. 83-93.
[38] Rene Voillaume, *Mitten in der Welt*, Vol. 65, Fribourg, 1960, p. 137.
[39] *Ibid.*, pp. 85, 92.
[40] Hauser, *op. cit.*, p. 147. Also consult Zeegers, *op. cit.*, p. 165.
[41] *Sexual Offenders and Social Punishment.* Evidence of the Church of England Moral Welfare Council, compiled and edited by D. S. Bailey, London, 1956, p. 96ff. Also *Homosexuality and Prostitution*, p. 91.
[42] *The Church's Mission Today*, pp. 6, 7. International Reformed Bulletin Nos. 20, 21, 22, Jan., Apr., July, 1965.
[43] Klaus Bockmuhl, *La Revue Reformee*, No. 62, 1965, Vol. XVI, p. 24. The writer is greatly indebted to Dr. Bockmuhl's article for the elucidation of his own thinking on a difficult subject.
[44] *Soundings*, edited by A. R. Vidler. H. A. Williams, *Theology and Self Awareness*, p. 80ff. For a brilliant critique of the new morality see Arnold Lunn's two books, *The New Morality* and the *Cult of Softness* (Blandford, London).
[45] Klaus Bockmuhl, La discussion sur l' Homosexualite. Point de vue theologique. *La Revue Reformee*, No. 62. 1965/2, Vol. XVI, p. 25.
[46] R. J. Rushdoony, *The Religion of Revolution.*
[47] C. H. and Winifred M. Whiteley, *The Permissive Morality* (Methuen, London, 1964), pp. 44, 132-5.
The reader who wishes to pursue further studies in this field should consult my work, *The Christian Philosophy of Law, Politics, and the State* (Presbyterian and Reformed Publishing Co.).